Beowulf and the Seventh Century

BEOWULF
AND
THE SEVENTH CENTURY

Language and Content

RITCHIE GIRVAN

with a new chapter by Rupert Bruce-Mitford

METHUEN & CO. LTD.

11 NEW FETTER LANE · LONDON EC4

First published 1935
Reissued with additional material 1971
© 1971 Methuen & Co Ltd
Chapter IV © 1971 Rupert Bruce-Mitford
Printed in Great Britain by
Butler & Tanner Ltd, Frome and London

Distributed in the U.S.A.
by Barnes & Noble Inc

PREFACE

FOR this reissue Professor Girvan's text has been reprinted without alteration. A new chapter, on the discoveries at Sutton Hoo, by Rupert Bruce-Mitford has been added together with a select bibliography by Christopher Ball, the archaeological section of which has been contributed by Dr. Bruce-Mitford.

In the original Edition of this book Professor Girvan wrote in his preface: 'These lectures are printed in the form in which they were delivered, with the exception that one or two paragraphs, which had to be curtailed or summarized, are here given in full. In the circumstances it was inevitable that conclusions should be stated without setting forth the evidence on which they are based, and it is impossible to do so now without rewriting the lectures, but the opportunity of printing permitted the addition of a few footnotes, chiefly in cases where a precise reference is intended, or a particular author or work mentioned.'

CONTENTS

I

THE LANGUAGE

IN the glossary to Klaeber's edition of *Beowulf* a useful attempt is made towards a classification of the vocabulary. Different symbols are prefixed to indicate words which occur only in *Beowulf*, those found only in poetry, and those found virtually only in one or the other, as well as for two other groups which may be left aside. There are in *Beowulf* rather more than thirty-one hundred distinct words, and almost thirteen hundred occur exclusively, or almost exclusively, in this poem and in the other poetical texts. Considerably more than one-third of the total vocabulary is alien from ordinary prose use. The proportion is somewhat startling and is responsible for a general impression that Anglo-Saxon poetry employs a special language, remote from ordinary usage, preserved by the activities of poets during the Anglo-Saxon period, and dying out completely when there were no longer poets to write or readers to read. If the notion that we have here a special language traditionally handed down were just, it must affect our judgment of its development, and in general of the laws which govern it, and conclusions drawn from the mass of the language in normal and habitual employment can be applied to it only with great reserve and at very considerable hazard. The impression derived from such statistics as those quoted is, however, entirely illusory. With some exceptions, which have their parallel in the poetry of every period, and, so far as I am aware, of every language, the vocabulary employed is essentially that of everyday use, or at all events of everyday literary use.

I begin a brief survey by glancing at the verb, for it is the skeleton of the sentence on which all the rest is supported. There are in round numbers three hundred and sixty uncompounded verbs in *Beowulf*, and forty of them are poetical words in the sense that they are unrecorded or rare in the existing prose writings. One hundred and fifty more occur with the prefix *ge-* (reckoning a few found only in the past-participle), but of these one hundred occur also as simple verbs, and the prefix is employed to render a shade of meaning which was perfectly known and thoroughly familiar except in the latest Anglo-Saxon period. It is not so much composition as what is in a way equivalent to an inflexion of the verb. Almost without exception they are moreover verbs in familiar use, though in a few cases the form with *ge-* is by chance recorded only in poetry. The remaining verbs are compounded with various prefixes and number two hundred. The prefixes are known and fertile in prose use, and in every case the sense is transparent, not to mention the fact that three-quarters of the total occur uncompounded in the poem. Sometimes the particular verb with the special prefix occurs only here or only in poetry, but it is evidently a matter of mere chance. In brief, of the verbs in *Beowulf* which are in any real sense alien from prose, the number approaches vanishing-point.

The nouns number sixteen hundred. Seven hundred of them, including those formed with prefixes, of which fifty (or considerably more than half) have *ge-*, are simple nouns. At the highest reckoning not more than one-fourth is absent in prose. That this is due in some degree to accident is

2

clear from the character of the words, and from the fact that several reappear and are common after the Norman Conquest. The nature of Anglo-Saxon prose literature forbids the possibility of our possessing a full record of the vocabulary in ordinary use. Moreover, such literature as we have is prevailingly southern, or later in a dialect determined by the spread of a κοινή based on West-Saxon. Thus the record is incomplete also in respect of time and place. There are large tracts of England of which we know nothing or next to nothing, and even in Northumbria, where we are more fortunately placed, there is a gap of more than two centuries between the scanty early remains and the later evidence, itself very one-sided in character. Making all allowance for these considerations, there is a considerable residue of words which seem clearly part of a poetical as distinct from a prose vocabulary. A large proportion is connected in a general way with war, and with the prince and his environment. These words may be archaisms inherited from early poetry, but it is impossible to tell from the evidence at our disposal whether they were archaisms or common terms of everyday speech at the end of the seventh century, a date for this poem defended by many scholars. The position is the same, and the same remarks apply to the adjectives. Out of a total of five hundred, two hundred are uncompounded, or if we add those with prefixes, the enormous majority having *ge-* or the negative *un-*, two hundred and seventy. I question if a dozen, certainly not more than a score, can be regarded as in any sense special to poetry, and I believe it may fairly be doubted if these were so at the beginning of the literary period. At all events, in both noun and adjective we are concerned with the retention of a small number of words which had passed out of current employment, and the position is similar to that we find in poetry at all periods. They were in fact familiar words, though not words we should use in ordinary speech or in ordinary prose. Words like *drēor*, ' shed blood ', or the adjective *drēorig*, were as well known to the Anglo-Saxon as *gore* and *gory* to the modern Englishman.

What does characterize Anglo-Saxon poetry is its fondness for compounds, compound nouns and compound adjectives. Of the nouns in *Beowulf* eight hundred and seventy are compound in the strict sense, of the adjectives two hundred and forty. This characteristic is not confined to Anglo-Saxon poetry ; it extends to all the Germanic languages, and beyond. In Anglo-Saxon it appears at all periods, early and late, though not quite in the same measure. It was a convention, as appears not least from the fact that frequently the compound adds little or nothing to the sense of the uncompounded word ; it was sought rather for the emotional value, and the presence of sounding compounds is throughout the mark of the poetic style. Here, too, it is necessary to examine the words more closely. An enormous proportion is marked as unknown outside of poetical texts, seven hundred and fifty and upwards out of a total of eight hundred and seventy nouns, and of the adjectives one hundred and ninety out of two hundred and forty. Over six hundred of the nouns are, however, compounded of elements familiar in prose. The residue is mainly formed by the incorporation of a few words very familiar in poetry, and has reference chiefly to war, arms, equipment and the like, or to the prince, his retinue, their relationship and activities. It is the same with the adjective. Most are compounded of common prose elements, and notably common are familiar formations in *-līc*, *-lēas*, *-fæst*, these numbering fifty of the whole. Compounds incorporating the few familiar poetic words *beadu-*, *gūð-*, *heaðu-*, *hild(e)-*, and the like, dealing with battle and its attendant circumstances, or with the retinue, account for most of the rest. I have emphasized this point because I wish to make clear that apart from

4

a mere handful of poetical archaisms, the vocabulary of *Beowulf* and the poetical vocabulary is what we meet elsewhere in Anglo-Saxon. The use to which it is put is different, but the elements are the same. It is a matter of some moment. We are entitled to assume that the language of poetry is bound by the same laws, subject to the same chronological changes. We have archaisms beyond all doubt, we have even more certainly dialecticism, but in the former case, where we are less well informed, we know enough to be sure that it is solely or almost solely a matter of vocabulary, of words, in the latter case we have the not inconsiderable evidence drawn from other sources to assist our determination of the provenance and history of the recorded form. There and in all other matters we can test the language against the evidence of other documents. The language of poetry is not *sui generis*, subject to rules of its own.

I have spoken hitherto of the content. Before I proceed to discuss the form, and the degree in which inferences from form are permissible, there are two points connected with content which have a bearing on the questions we are concerned to settle. Anglo-Saxon has at all times great freedom in the making and use of compounds, but there is a difference, and the difference may suggest chronological conclusions. In normal prose use compound nouns and adjectives are markedly fewer compared with uncompounded. This is very noticeable in the adjective where the impression of relative frequency is due to the enormous extension of adjectives in *-līc*, a suffix which in later employment often adds little or nothing to the sense. This extension of the suffix evidently began early, and we have numerous instances in all verse texts, but nothing comparable with the prose use. It seems to be a fact also that in late (tenth-century) verse the proportion of simple and compound approximates more nearly to that of prose.

5

The point must not be pressed, for much depends on subject, and statistics could and would give a deceptive result. It cannot be gainsaid, however, that *Beowulf* occupies a quite exceptional position. The preponderance of compound forms is marked, and I believe in no other Anglo-Saxon poem does a similar relation exist. The nearest amongst those I have tested are *Andreas,* an obvious imitation of *Beowulf,* the *Older Genesis,* and, in regard to the noun, *Exodus,* and in all of them the uncompounded forms prevail considerably. This is one of many points in which *Beowulf* occupies an isolated position in Anglo-Saxon literature. Another point may be associated with it in that respect, I mean the adjectival compounds in which the second element is a noun, the so-called bahuvrīhi compounds. This is a well-known Indo-European formation, but the original type is already restricted in Germanic, and rapidly becoming still more restricted in Anglo-Saxon. I exclude from consideration adjectives in -*līc,* though in origin they belong to the group. The suffix became fertile at an early date, later extremely so, and soon lost the characteristic sense, ' possessing ' or ' possessed of something '. I exclude also such as have adverbial prefixes or particles, which in any case are rare in poetry, and a few others for one reason or another, because they are really substantives, or because of a measure of doubt in their explanation. Several of the kind defined occur in early glossaries or in prose as well as in poetry, but there is a tendency from the beginning to substitute a *j*-form with consequential mutation, and still later to employ participial forms, e.g. *hwīt-fōt,* ' white-footed ', as compared with *fyðer-fēte,* ' four-footed ', or again *hwīt-locc* besides *hwīt-locced,* ' white-haired '. In later prose very few appear, chiefly -*mōd,* which was very fertile, and -*heort.* In *Beowulf* we are in touch with a period when this method of composition was still living, if decaying, and it is employed freely. We find sixteen separate formations involving thirty-five different words. Some may be and doubtless are inherited, some give the impression of being invented for the occasion. There is nothing comparable elsewhere in Anglo-Saxon poetry. The nearest approach in extent of use is in the *Older Genesis* with nine formations in twenty-five words, *Andreas* with six in twenty-two. Of formations not in *Beowulf* there are two in *Genesis*, one in *Exodus*, and seven in *The Riddles*. The other poems content themselves almost exclusively, it would seem, with repeating the familiar expressions, especially those which survived in prose. On both counts, the preponderance of *composita* and the free employment of bahuvrīhi adjectives, *Beowulf* stands apart from other Anglo-Saxon poems, and there is a suggestion —I do not claim it as more—that it stands apart because it is at or represents an earlier stage of the language. I turn to consider it as to form, i.e. with regard to admixture due to dialect or chronology.

Anglo-Saxon, when we become acquainted with it in the earliest records, shows numerous dialectal differences, but the differences are neither old nor profound. Bede's tribal distinction, Jutes, Saxons, and Angles, is familiar, familiar too is a grouping of dialects which corresponds more or less with the tribal distribution, Kentish, Saxon, and Anglian. These names suggest that the dialects are based on tribal differences, and implicitly that they reflect a pre-conquest condition. It is not so. Dialect groups in Anglo-Saxon England are determined by geographical proximity. Not a single point of divergence can be proved to belong to a pre-conquest period, and there is none which is not with probability to be assigned to a period after the settlement. Tribal differences may have existed, but we do not know what they were, and they must have been negligible. The important developments in Anglo-Saxon are essentially in common, with slight variations in detail.   One of the most important, the *i*-mutation, which profoundly modified the sound and appearance of the language, was in the seventh century relatively recent ; others were then in process of development.   We have a good deal of information about England at that time. Bede notes a point of divergence between his native Northumbrian and the language of Wessex,[1] but he never gives a hint that there was the slightest difficulty of communication over the whole country.   Eddius in the contemporary life of Wilfrid mentions no difficulty of language in Mercia, or even in Sussex, Wessex, and Kent.   Moreover, to go farther afield, Wilfrid and other English missionaries do not seem to have met any serious impediment in a difference of language among Frisians, Saxons on the Continent, even, it would appear, Danes in Jutland.   It is true that we learn from Bede that Coinualch of Wessex quarrelled and parted with his Frankish bishop, tired of his barbarous speech.[2]   If Agilberct spoke Frankish, and that is not certain, it is still to be remembered that Frankish is at a considerable remove from Anglo-Saxon, and Bede's words do not of necessity imply that Coinualch could not understand him.   At all events, at a time when intercourse with foreign peoples presented little difficulty, it may safely be assumed that in England there was no difficulty at all. We have a picture in *Widsith* of the *scop* wandering from court to court, reciting his lays to the various audiences as he found them, and receiving his reward according as he pleased his patrons.   The picture is in line with other evidence, and, as is well known, the heroic material had in the true sense neither home nor fatherland ; it was the common property of all.   Such a condition is not reconcilable with a difficulty, or even a limitation, inherent in mutual intercourse, but more than that, it has a distinct bearing on the linguistic habits of the poet.   Words, forms, and usages from diverse dialects could be, and doubtless

[1] *Hist. Eccl.* II. v.   [2] *Ibid.* III. vii.

were, incorporated in the language of poetry. There was a stock of terms, phrases, modes of expression, common to all heroic poetry in all Germanic languages, and the common possession of all makers of heroic poetry. They lay ready to hand and passed without change into religious poetry. We have to approach the study of *Beowulf* with these facts in mind, remembering especially that dialectal inconsistency, and in some degree chronological inconsistency, are to be expected in a linguistic tradition so developed. It must also be remembered that the language of poetry was the possession of every Anglo-Saxon of a certain class—I will not say educated or lettered, for these are bookish words—and that the knowledge evidently extended beyond that class. On the dialect element the only limitation was one of actual convenience. Extreme forms would normally be avoided. On the chronological mixture this much may be said. Obviously there can be admixture of old and new, but except at a period on the limits of both, when the old is antiquated but known—I refer to grammatical forms, not to words—the old will occur only in formulae and conventional phrases.

Our manuscript of *Beowulf* is at several removes from the original. That is beyond all dispute. There are omissions, errors, and confusions which can have arisen only in the course of transmission through a series of copyists. Some of the variant dialect forms which appear in the text are with great probability to be charged to the different scribes who copied it out, and very many of the chronologically discrepant forms and inflexions are beyond doubt due to their activities. These facts are in line with the history of all the manuscripts we know. Late forms occur side by side with others which are not usual in late texts or are even definitely early. It is important to settle the question how far any late forms can

9

be claimed as original in the text, for if demonstrably
late forms occur and are essential to sense or metre, either
we have deliberate reconstruction of the verse, or else
the poem is not earlier than the date of their first appearance. I do not say that 'the date of appearance can be
determined with exactness or in some instances at all,
but there are cases where it can be given approximately
within certain limits. It can be said at once, however,
that it is always a mere matter of spelling, or of forms and
inflexions which are indifferent from the point of view of
grammar and metre. I do not think there is any example
of an essential form which can be maintained as really
late. Some which have been so explained should be rejected. The neuter accusative plural of the adjective in
-e is late, but *fāge* in line 1615 is probably feminine singular ;
and *sinnihte* in line 161, which has been explained as
dative singular of *sinniht*, is late if rightly explained, but
it is really accusative singular of a *j*-stem neuter *sinnihte*.
There are some probable or possible cases of the accusative
singular of feminine *i*-stem nouns in *-e* which have been
cited as late. In particular words the old endingless
accusative was long maintained, but in others the new
form was early, perhaps earliest in compounds. In *dǣd*,
the most significant case for *Beowulf*, it is dialectically
ninth-century or earlier. Accordingly it would still be
inadmissible to explain these as late, even if all the instances could not be otherwise interpreted, namely, as
accusative plural. The evidence of language does not
justify the assumption of a late, i.e. a tenth-century origin,
though at the same time the absence of late forms does
not prove that the poem is earlier. The question of early
forms will occupy us presently. Meantime let us not forget
that old and new can coexist even in current speech.
We have in Modern English *thou* and *thee* beside *you*,
blessed beside *blest*. The nature of the discourse determines their employment. *Thou* would be an archaism in

scribed, the only original dialect traces on which we can depend are such as are due to a blunder or misunderstanding of the scribés, and these rest in the end on conjecture. Such have been assumed in *þēod*, l. 1278, for *dēað*, perhaps in *fēla*, l. 1032, and in *gang*, which occurs three times for *gēong*, ' went ', supposed to have been mistaken for a noun. All are Northumbrian, but the first is the only one really probable. There are other forms like *geþah* in l. 1024 which are in general poetic use and prove nothing. The number of significant instances is excessively small. If on the other hand a dialect form is regularly maintained, no matter whence it comes, it must be because it is part of the accepted language of poetry, of the poetic convention. This is true, for instance, of unsyncopated verb-forms. It is perhaps only in the strictest West-Saxon that these are the rule. Some, but slight, conclusions may be drawn from the absence of particular dialect characteristics, but our relative ignorance of the habits of many dialects in early times, in later times, or in both, forbids dogmatism.

In view of the considerations set forth we may well ask whether it is possible to draw any conclusions of date or dialect from the language of the poem as handed down to us. In attempting an answer we are faced with a preliminary question. Are we dealing with a poem written down from the beginning or transmitted for some part of its descent by oral tradition ? The question is difficult, and the answer to it must in part depend on aesthetic judgment with which we have here no concern. The following points have, however, some weight. Any who believe in oral tradition in its strict interpretation must also hold that our poem is an accretion, that the last to handle the matter has incorporated with no essential change large portions of the work of numerous predecessors, for if the last to treat the subject made the poem anew from

colloquial speech and in normal literary use, but
living form in a particular limited sphere. The lan
of literature is always in some degree an abstra
It crystallizes the habits of a period at least
remove from current use, and the language of po
is merely a slight exaggeration of an habitual lite
practice.

The question of the introduction of dialect forms in t
transmission of the text is closely connected with the da
of composition or at least of the first writing, and for th
moment can only be answered provisionally. One strikin
characteristic of the language is the prevalence of the back-
mutation of *a*, whereby arises the diphthong *ea*. In the
poem words with regular or occasional *a* are known in
prose, those specifically poetical have *ea*. In two early
glossaries, Epinal and Erfurt, which represent the language
of the early eighth century (and earlier), the prerequisite
for the mutation is known, but not the mutation itself.
The Corpus glossary, which may reflect the linguistic
habits of the later eighth century, but not earlier, has the
mutation freely, and in original charters it appears about
the end of the century. The development seems to belong
to the later eighth century. It is also locally restricted,
neither West-Saxon nor Northumbrian, but Mercian, and
perhaps South-East Mercian, with some extension in the
neighbouring Kentish. There is but one example in the
eighth-century manuscripts of Bede, in Cotton Tib. C. ii,
which has linguistic affinities with the South-East. The
Northumbrian *Liber Vitae* has numerous examples of the
diphthong, but as the dialect does not show the change
early or late, or yet the fronting of *a* which made it
possible, the names can hardly be Northumbrian. Those
who believe that *Beowulf* is early or Northumbrian must
also believe that the diphthong was introduced in the
process of copying. If the poem is early and often tran-

beginning to end, and we have his work as he made it, that is for our purpose identical with one written from the first. I shall touch on the question of oral transmission later on (see pp. 31 ff.). Meantime it is enough to say that the Germanic *scop* was primarily a maker, who made a new poem on the basis of old material, and that the idea of traditional transmission except in phrase or epithet is a delusion. The extent of the poem is another argument in support of the view that it was at once committed to writing. It is difficult to see how otherwise it could have been preserved. The mere bulk sets it apart from all heroic lays of which we have trace. It could never have been recited in hall in its complete form, and it cannot easily be divided into sections suitable for delivery there. Moreover, it is too leisurely, and lacks the packed dramatic intensity which is characteristic of the lays and had evidently a special appeal. Finally, the fact that it has numbered sections which are evidently old, and probably original, strongly suggests a literary composition in the strict sense. If it owes any debt to the Cædmonian poetry, as is likely, or to Virgil, as has been claimed, then it is incredible that it was not conceived as a work of literature. If this conclusion is well founded, then we are dealing with a written work, and that the work of an individual poet, as individual as Cynewulf, and we are accordingly justified in making inferences as to the original form and date, and in stating positive conclusions, if we can.

The dialect of poetry is mainly what we call Anglian, that is to say, it has characteristics in form and vocabulary which we can parallel from Anglian territory and not elsewhere. This can hardly be due to anything but that the models were Anglian. Most of the surviving poetry is Christian religious poetry, and we have the definite statement of Bede that the type originated in Northumbria,

13

also that it was imitated elsewhere,[1] and what is preserved
is in many cases suggestive of Northumbria. This must
have had a strong influence on the traditional language.
The earlier texts were of course subjected to the usual
influences in the course of their descent, some alteration
in spelling and inflexion, and the introduction of alien
dialectal elements, for none is preserved in a form even
approximately Northumbrian. The successive scribes copy
with reasonable fidelity, but it is certain that there is a
persistent impulse to alter into the familiar, and that it
acts continuously on words and forms not consecrated by
poetic convention. It is certain, too, that the scribes do
not consciously preserve archaic forms. They are smoothed
out as the text passes from scribe to scribe. What remains and is recognizable may well be regarded as legiti-
mately admissible in poetry. In seeking origins we are
again dependent on blunders and misunderstandings. It
is possible, and I think probable, that we have one such
in *hrærg* for *hærg* in l. 175. The anticipation of *r* is a
common type of textual error, but that need not concern us further. Once miswritten, it was copied mechani-
cally and preserved because no longer understood. If the
scribe had understood the word he would have made it
herg or *hearg* as it appears elsewhere, but by an accident
we can restore an older and more original spelling. The
Epinal and Erfurt glossaries have *e* from *æ*, but the change
was known to their dialect under other conditions and
proves nothing. The Corpus glossary has normally *æ*,
once *e* in a word not in Epinal-Erfurt, and apparently
belongs to the period of change, for the general development to *e* does not occur there. It is hazardous to base
conclusions on these glossaries alone, for the dialect may
be mixed, but a date in the later eighth century appears
to be confirmed by the evidence of charters. If that is
sound, *hærg* is not later than the early eighth century,

---

[1] *Hist. Eccl.* IV. xxiv.

and may be earlier.   It is a small point, but not without significance.[1]

Another means employed for the restoration of archaic forms is the evidence of metre.   Here we are on more debatable ground.   The looseness of the metrical scheme permits variation in form not to be detected by any test at our disposal.   The scribes undoubtedly altered the texts in transmission, and could bring the metre into conformity with later habits where necessary, and that would be in a minority of instances.   Moreover, abnormal metrical types consequential on change could be and were regarded as admissible licence and imitated later.   In any event we are concerned only with variation in the total quantity of words, or in the distribution of the quantity, and that as measured metrically, i.e. with syllabic loss in syncope and apocope, with compensatory lengthening, with the introduction of inorganic vowels involving syllabic increase. The total quantity of the word has a direct relation to the metrical scheme, and conclusions can sometimes be drawn from the text of *Beowulf* as to the presence or absence of the linguistic developments mentioned.   If in fact we found something in conflict with the practice of the rest of Anglo-Saxon poetry, important conclusions would be justified, but the cases in which we are so happily placed are excessively rare.   What we should like is evidence that *Beowulf* kept and demanded old forms while other or most other poems did not admit them.   We do not get it.   Our evidence taken at the best is negative. One point may be selected to illustrate.   The present subjective of the substantive verb appears both as monosyllable and as disyllable.   The original singular form was

---

[1] A less likely survival is *ǣg*- in *ǣgweard* (l. 241) beside *ēg*- in *ēgstrēam* (l. 577) and (blundered) *ecgclif* (l. 2893).   Other explanations are possible.

sī. In time the ordinary subjunctive ending was added, making a disyllable *sī-æ*. At a third stage the vowels coalesced into a diphthong, so becoming again monosyllabic. We do not know the date of the successive changes, except that Bede in 735 has the disyllable,[1] nor can we tell whether the variation in *Beowulf* is between the first stage and the second, or between second and third, while lastly, the word is measured metrically both as monosyllable and disyllable in other poems. It can, I believe, be shown that *Beowulf* is later than syncope and apocope, but that in itself tells us little unless we can point to some datable poetry which is earlier, and that we cannot do, or can establish a date more or less precise for the development itself, which to some extent we can do. That alone is nothing. At most we get an upper limit ; later could mean centuries later.

It is an elementary fact of Anglo-Saxon grammar that in the consonantal groups *rh*, *lh*, the *h* is lost when the group is intervocalic, with consequential lengthening of a preceding short vowel. Later the original short vowel or diphthong was sometimes reintroduced from forms where *h* remained. In *Beowulf* there are supposed to be three instances of this restoration which obviously must be later and perhaps considerably later than loss and lengthening. All three are in the one word *feorh*. Two of them, it seems to me, can quite well be long (ll. 73, 1843), the other is short but occurs in a phrase which then and later was a virtual adverb,[2] and may well owe its quantity to early reduction under a single accent in the manner usual in such phrases. A general inference is not warranted. There is the question of contraction. Some words have very early contraction and the few disyllabic forms which occur can readily be explained by analogical addition of

---

[1] *Death Song*, l. 2.   [2] *tō wīdan feore* l. 933.

the usual endings. Such is *frēa*, which as a first element in composition is probably always a monosyllable (as it ought to be), but in inflexion in a minority of instances disyllabic. I confine attention to contraction due to loss of *h*, because we have early texts with uncontracted forms, in which it is also possible that the *h* was not yet silent. The examples are in glossaries and may be inherited, but the original cannot be very early in the seventh century. Of verb forms in *Beowulf* the large majority either must be or can be disyllabic ; the explanation of the remainder as monosyllabic depends on our judgment of the metre. If we admit that the prefix *ge-* can be an anacrusis in the second half-line, as it is in a few unrelated instances, four can be disyllabic, three more if we exclude inorganic vowels, the last only if we admit an abnormal metrical type. Nouns, adjectives, and adverbs show greater variation, but in most cases the admission of an anacrusis makes a disyllable necessary, including four where a needless demonstrative may have been introduced by the scribe. There is a small residue involving abnormal metre. The numeral *tȳn* occurs once as an evident monosyllable. It would be easy to amend this line also, but I am not concerned to suggest alterations in the text in any, and we may grant that contraction was known, though exceptional. A similar condition is found in several poems which on other grounds have claims to be early, e.g. *Exodus, Genesis, Guthlac A*, while it appears that in the works of Cynewulf, dated more or less precisely in the later eighth century, contraction is almost universal. On the other hand, uncontracted forms occur in poetry which is demonstrably late, and analogical addition of the normal endings in verb, noun, and adjective is easy and frequent in prose as well as verse. The influence of a conventional phraseology and a stereotyped metrical form is a factor of importance. Nevertheless, making all allowance for the influence of poetic style, in *Beowulf* and some other poems the uncontracted forms are hardly a convention, and especially the extent of their employment suggests that it and they are close to the period of change.

Decisive evidence in the matter of inorganic vowels is difficult, perhaps impossible, of attainment ; it depends too much on our subjective judgment of the metre, as is evident enough from the remarks on contraction. We must allow a few cases where the inorganic vowel is present ; some words are metrically indifferent, in others it depends on the admissible metrical types. If certain metrical types are illegitimate, we can obtain normal verses by excluding inorganic vowels, and we should have in *Beowulf* accordingly a condition in which the vowel can be present or absent. On the other hand, we must then extend the exclusion occasionally to words where the vowel is radical and habitually retained. On the whole, therefore, it is more probable that the doubtful metrical types were regarded as a permissible licence, the vowel lightly pronounced, and the metrical type itself inherited from a period before the development of the inorganic vowel, and that the licence was by analogy extended to other words with radical vowel. That means that the period of development was not only in the past but in a not immediate past, and the conclusion is confirmed by the fact that words in which, after the introduction of the new vowel, the syllabic quantity is invariable, appear to have the vowel without exception. It is true that some texts of the early eighth century, e.g. the early glossaries, have examples without secondary vowel, but these are certainly either inherited or analogically reconstructed.

Finally, when we consider apocope and syncope the matter is plain. To reintroduce apocopated and syncopated vowels would mean little less than rewriting the poem. If grammatical inferences on relative historical development have any validity, then the syncope of *æ*, *e* was later than *i*-mutation, and more or less contemporaneous with syncope of *i*, *u* (perhaps a little earlier), and the insertion of both groups, and even of the latter, would destroy the metre. Another point may be mentioned. The word *hild*, feminine *jō*-stem, has two combining forms, *hilde*- and *hild*-, the latter only before a short syllable but always there. The only reasonable explanation is that the distinction came into being at the period of apocope. It is without parallel in Anglo-Saxon, and the grounds for it need not be discussed here. All other words of its class have but one combining form, determined by the nominative singular with its regular loss of vowel, and compared with *hilde*- an innovation. That is also the condition in *Beowulf*, and the conclusion cannot be escaped that the period of origin of the double form, i.e. the period of apocope, was not only past but long past. It is a survival, maintaining itself in poetry and in proper names after the governing principle had been forgotten and the distinction obliterated. Perhaps I may add that in my opinion the syncope and apocope belong to the earlier half of the seventh century. Bede, for instance, gives the name of the famous abbess at Whitby as Hild, and there is no reason to doubt that that was what she called herself. She was born in 614 and died in 680. I am suggesting, accordingly, that our evidence proves *Beowulf* later than these, later also than the introduction of inorganic vowels, and that its relation to contraction points to a period when these changes were in progress or recent.

In 1906 Lorenz Morsbach examined existing records with the aim of fixing a precise date for the apocope of *u* and the loss of *h*.[1] The date on which he determined is in the

---

[1] *Zur Datierung des Beowulf-epos* in *Nachr. der kgl. Gesell. der Wiss zu Göttingen. Phil.-Hist. Klasse* (1906), pp. 252–77.

end based on two words, the personal name *Uelhisci* in a
Kentish Charter of 679,[1] and *flodu* on the Franks Casket,
assigned to *c.* 700, where respectively *h* remained and *u*
was not apocopated. Too much stress can be laid on the
spelling of a single name in a charter. It may represent
the archaic spelling of an older generation, and in this
particular instance the analogy of *Wealh* cannot be ex-
cluded. Nevertheless, it is quite possible that it was a
living use, and the loss of *h* may well be later than 679.
Intervocalic *h* cannot have been lost much before 700, and
the other does not seem to have been earlier. Bede writes
an uncontracted *Treenta*, ' Trent ' (beside *Treanta*), and
contraction cannot have been long after loss. This point,
however, does not prove much for *Beowulf*, and Morsbach's
demonstration rests really on the Franks Casket. If one
is to base conclusions on a single form there are certain
conditions which it must satisfy. The form must be
beyond suspicion of tampering, the grammatical explanation must be beyond all doubt, and, if chronology is in
question, the date must be certain. Clearly the first condition is satisfied, much less certainly the second and third.
The date is not ascertainable except that it is not earlier
than the second half of the seventh century nor later than
the first half of the eighth. It is true that the chances
are against a sporadic occurrence ; on the other hand, the
evidence of the monument must be taken as a whole. As
to the second condition, I cannot agree that the grammatical explanation is certain. I shall not discuss other
possible explanations, but approach the matter from a
different angle. As far as grammatical investigation can
determine, the relative order of phonological changes affect-
ing the question is as follows : (1) Apocope and Syncope,
(2) inorganic vowels, (3) smoothing of diphthongs, (4a) loss
of intervocalic *h*, (4b) loss of *h* in *rh*, *lh*, (5a) contraction,
and (5b) compensatory lengthening. Smoothing was per-

---

[1] W. de G. Birch, *Cart. Sax.* no. 45.

haps in progress during 2, and 2 in progress during 1. Now the Franks Casket has certainly 2 and 3, and, in spite of Morsbach's special pleading, with great probability 4*b* and 5*b*. It seems incredible that it has not also 1, Apocope. The only sort of answer that I can see is that there was a long interval between the apocope of *i* and the apocope of *u*, for we have clear evidence on the Casket that *i* had not only been lost but that subsequent change had occurred. It is true that *u* throughout its history is more resistant to loss than *i*, but the assumption that there was a long interval, and that at the close of the seventh century, is one to which the grammarian cannot assent. It contradicts all the evidence at our disposal which is supported by a marked parallelism in treatment. If *u* had indeed remained down to 700 we could hardly have failed to find further evidence in early texts.

It is worth considering the evidence which we can deduce from the Casket. In the first place we have the name *Ægili* with a final *i* later lost. We must not assume that in such position *i* disappeared at the same time as in disyllabic words. I set beside it the adjective *æðele*, a rare type of formation in Anglo-Saxon, and probably an *i*-stem which should have become **æðel* but retains *e* by influence of the *ja*-stem adjectives. Both words appear in composition in two spellings, with initial *Æ* and initial *E*. An identical variation appears in the name *Ætla, Etla*, Anglo-Saxon forms of *Attila*, and the former can be and has been explained as due to late borrowing. The explanation will not do for *Ægil*, which place-names prove to be early. I assume a suffix variation **aʒili* as in the fourth-century name *Agilimundus*,[1] and **aʒuli, *aþili* and **aþuli* because it is only by such *u*- forms that the initial

[1] *Ammiani Marcellini Rerum Gestarum libri*, ed. C. U. Clark (Berlin 1910), I, p. 128 (Bk. XVII, cap. 12, § 21).

Æ can be explained,[1] and *u* for Germanic *a* (or rather *o*)
is widely spread in Anglo-Saxon under certain conditions.
Now we have coins of Æthelred of Mercia with runic in-
scriptions in the two forms *Æþiliræd* and *Æþilræd*. As we
can hardly imagine the name as built with two different
elements we must conclude that one is an earlier, the other
a later, spelling. His regnal years are 675–704. It is likely
that he so spelled his name within the limits of his reign,
and at all events his lifetime must have coincided with
the change. He cannot have been born much before 650.
Bede and Eddius mention his name often, but always in
the later form. Little weight can be given to the manuscripts of Eddius, and it is likely enough that the early
form survived till near the end of the century.

I do not propose to dwell on the significance of *Giuþeasu*
except to remark that once we admit the idea of blunders
(putting aside the cryptogrammic portion) we destroy the
foundation on which we build, and when we allow deliberate
omissions owing to lack of space, we display ignorance of
the method of skilled craftsmen putting together and
adorning a costly and valued work of art. Two other
points, however, claim a word. We have, if Napier's
explanation of *fergen* is right, one example of *e* for un-
stressed *i*. The first *e* is surprising in face of *firgin* in the
early glossaries, yet I have noted in a tenth-century Charter [2]
æt Feregenne, the modern Ferryhill in Durham, which
Stephens long ago wished to identify with the Casket's
fergenberig. The etymology of *twægen* is obscure and we
do not know certainly what *e* represents, most probably
earlier *æ*. The first recorded instance of *e* for *i* is in an

---

[1] There is a bare possibility, which I have left aside, that the
vowel is long. The treatment in early OE of trisyllables with a long
vowel followed by *i* in two successive syllables, when the penult is
short, is difficult and obscure.

[2] W. de G. Birch, *Cart. Sax.* no. 1256.

Essex Charter of 692–3,[1] and the change of *æ* was in general earlier. An Essex Charter does not prove the same date for Northumbria, and the Casket otherwise has unchanged *æ* and *i*. The Northern change is associated with the early eighth century, and glossaries and charters show that it cannot be much earlier elsewhere. If these facts are worthy of trust, the usual dating of the Franks Casket cannot be far wrong, but it makes it incredible that it belongs to a period when apocope had not occurred. The series of subsequent developments, which are all also before the date of our texts, demands no inconsiderable time. We must accordingly reject the view that evidence of the date of apocope can be derived from the Casket, except in the sense that it also is subsequent to it, and that in forms like *Ægili* the vowel lingered late, as old forms often do in personal names.

The syntactical evidence has been discussed so often that I may be permitted to deal with it in a few sentences. The things emphasized are the use of the demonstrative in its original function, and not as an article, and the employment of the weak adjective. There is no doubt that in *Beowulf* the demonstrative force of the pronoun is present in a greater degree than in other poems, and that it is at a farther remove from prose in that respect. It is also true that in regard to the weak adjective without preceding demonstrative there is a startling discrepancy between *Beowulf* and the rest. On the other hand, it is not true that the use as article is absent, nor can a logical employment be established for the weak adjective. It is easy to show that it has a meaning where it is found, but it is not found in all places where, if logically used, it ought to be. From the facts the only possible conclusion is that the new usages were known but rare, and it is difficult to resist the inference that they are notably rarer in *Beowulf*

[1] W. de G. Birch, *Cart. Sax.* no. 81. Cf. A. H. Smith, *Three Northumbrian Poems*, p. 35.

because it is older. A close investigation of syntactical usages might lead to results of great value for both date and dialect, but I doubt greatly if we have the material on which alone such a study can be based.

The results we have got for the date of *Beowulf* in this investigation of the linguistic evidence are not impressive. It is clear that it occupies an isolated position in some matters of vocabulary and syntax, and most probably because it is earlier than other Anglo-Saxon poems, at least in the form in which they have descended. It can be established that it is considerably later than syncope and apocope, and made probable that it is later than the introduction of inorganic vowels ; it has been suggested, though it cannot be demonstrated, that it belongs to the period of contraction or just after, while older forms survived in the language of poetry, even if the new were already habitual in speech. The oldest of these phonological changes, syncope and apocope, belongs to the earlier seventh century, and the introduction of inorganic vowels probably followed hard upon it. They give us accordingly little help in fixing a precise date, for *Beowulf* must in any case be later than the middle of the seventh century. Christianity is in the fabric, and if, as is likely, it originated in more northerly England, it is impossible that it was written till well after 650, even making allowance for the astonishing speed with which Christianity rooted itself in Northumbria. The relation to contraction indicates a date at or very little after 700. Two little points of evidence may be mentioned here. One is the use of *nōn* as a familiar measure of time, in fact as the hour when men ate. As the form shows, the word was borrowed in England after the introduction of Christianity ; its use and spread are unquestionably due to the important office of the church celebrated at that hour. If we allow time for naturalization as a term of common speech, we cannot assume a

24

date too close to the conversion of Northumbria. The other point has reference to the word *gīgant*, used of the giants who warred with God. It was never a familiar word in Anglo-Saxon. A very late writer thought it necessary to explain it with the gloss *ent*, and it occurs but rarely in the texts and always with the same scriptural reference. Our author must have got it from the biblical story ; it is a plausible conjecture that he owes it to the original Cædmonian poems. The subject would have attracted the Germanic poet, and the name remains even in our so-called *Older Genesis*. I am suggesting that *Beowulf* is later than Cædmon, not earlier, that is, than about 670. If I had to fix a date for its composition within reasonable limits, I should decide for 680–700. That was the period when Northumbria was at the height of its greatness politically and artistically ; it was also the period when it was on the edge of decline. Both greatness and decay appear to me mirrored in the intellectual and moral atmosphere. It will be worth while to trace whether, and if so how far, our knowledge of the conditions in the later seventh century is reflected in the poem.

II

THE BACKGROUND

NONE in these days disputes that *Beowulf* is an English poem. Views may differ as to the time and manner in which it assumed its present shape, but all theories of translation are abandoned. An interesting light on the accepted attitude is apparent in a fairly recent study by Schücking, which at bottom is an attempt to combine the old view of Danish origin with English composition.[1] That we need not discuss. Since the poem is English it ought not to be impossible to bring it into relation with some particular stage of Anglo-Saxon development, for it must have a background in time and place, and this will betray itself, however much it owes to tradition. If we could set it in some precisely defined environment, it would go far to settle questions of date and provenance. I do not say it can be done in a manner to allay doubt or silence criticism, but striking analogies can be found, and these from the time which linguistic evidence led us to assume as a probable date.

The historical events in *Beowulf* belong in and around the early decades of the sixth century. It may be taken for granted that the knowledge was transmitted to later times in heroic lays, and that the original lays were nearly contemporary with the events. From them or their successors *Beowulf* draws its information, and the question

---

[1] Paul u. Braune's *Beitr. zur Geschichte der deutschen Spr. u. Lit.* xlvii. 293 ff.

at once arises whether it has retained material from the early sixth century in an unaltered form. It is a question which cannot be put by. It is often, perhaps universally, assumed that *Beowulf* carries us back directly to the time of the migrations. It has been set alongside Tacitus as a witness of the Germanic period, and it is not surprising, for it is the most important Germanic document in extent and character which we possess. Seebohm based upon it inferences on the conduct and limitations of the blood-feud ;[1] more significant still, Knut Stjerna sets it side by side with the results of archaeological investigation in Scandinavia and draws on the statements in the poem to illustrate the finds, and on these to supplement, or occasionally explain and correct, the statements in the poem.[2] Many proceed on the assumption that *Beowulf* can be used unreservedly to throw light on Germanic habits. Are we to assume that the conditions are those of the early sixth century, or, on the other hand, conditions familiar in the poet's lifetime, and, with some obvious exceptions traditionally maintained, Germanic only when and in so far as the two coincided ? It is well to remember that the gap is less than two centuries, if conclusions drawn from language are just, but they were centuries full of movement and development. In some vital respects the difference was profound. I regard with grave doubt the habit of equating *Beowulf* with the early sixth century, or with any period earlier than the date of composition. In matters which have place or reference in the poem we may find it necessary to distinguish between concrete objects which could survive, and those conditions, practices, and habits which the poet could know only by hearsay, and in comparing *Beowulf* with the life of the seventh century in England we shall have to consider whether it agrees in all respects

[1] F. Seebohm, *Tribal Custom in Anglo-Saxon Law* (1911), pp. 56 ff.
[2] *Essays on Beowulf*, ed. and tr. by J. R. Clark Hall (Viking Society 1912).

or in all essential respects, or whether in some important details it is at odds, with the records of that time.

Linguistic evidence forbids the assumption that we have sixth-century material, or as I believe material earlier than the later seventh century, intact. Any survivals in phrase or epithet are brought into line with the later form of the language, and original matter must of necessity have been rehandled. That in itself does not exclude the possibility of accuracy in detail. In special circumstances an accurate picture of a past period with obsolete cultural conditions can be preserved for centuries, and not only when there is no linguistic breach. A comparison of such circumstances with those prevailing in Germanic antiquity may prove illuminating. I think of two illustrative examples and begin with the nearer. In Ireland the Ulster epic cycle, originating about the first century of the Christian era, preserves without essential change, though in altered language, a picture of obsolete conditions. There was, however, in Ireland long before Christianity was introduced a school of scholars and poets, the *fili*, in charge of profane learning. They were earnest students of ancient lore, including the language in which it was preserved. In the seventh century the initiate were still in possession of an esoteric language which the tyro did not yet know, and this can only have been obsolete forms, expressions, and words of the earlier period as preserved in the epic stories. A friendly relation was maintained after the introduction of Christianity between Church and *fili*, and our knowledge of Old Irish is due to the interest of the clergy in the language. The astonishing development of scholarship in Ireland can, I believe, be attributed in no small degree to this pre-existing tradition of scholarship. Such a professional school can transmit by oral tradition text or content unchanged. The early adoption of the roman script gave to the stories the chance of being committed to writing in pagan form, with suppressions in the interests of Christian doctrine, but with no introduction of Christian ideas and influence. One of the main occupations of the *fili* was the memorizing and retailing of stories, and primarily old stories. In characteristic Celtic fashion the members of the body, and the stories too, were divided into numerous classes, the former according to the number of stories they possessed, at the head the *ollamh* with two hundred and fifty greater and one hundred lesser, and a story in O'Curry,[1] where a *file* suggests several to a king to have them all rejected in turn as familiar, postulates essential identity in form. It is true that the story of Cuchulain is not preserved in the language in which it must first have been composed, and that is due to the profound changes in form which took place during those early centuries and altered it out of recognition. If the story was to be understood, it had of necessity to be modernized to keep pace with linguistic development. The words had not that fixity of form characteristic of Greek, nor could there be till much later a syllabic metre of rigid form. Nevertheless, the vital features of the epic could be and were preserved, the spirit of the past and the picture of the civilization.

The second example is Homer, and there we have the advantage of a language surviving in a form traditional but intelligible, subject only to minor alteration. The close similarity, or rather identity, with conditions in the Mycenaean or Sub-Mycenaean age necessitates a date when it was still a living memory. Part at least must have been inherited, and I do not see how it can have been handed down, unless there was a body of professionals who transmitted unchanged what they had received, the *Homeridae* of Greek tradition, cultivators and reciters of Homeric poetry. Epic style and fixity of metre help con-

[1] E. [O']Curry, *Manners and Customs of the Ancient Irish*, II. 131.

siderably, but are not in themselves sufficient to explain the consistency of the account. What is in question is the casual, unconscious indication, the assumption of a familiar knowledge which needs no explanation. I think of the story of Troy told by Odysseus in *Odyssey* xiv (a book believed by many to be late), where the equipment is taken for granted, for example, where the men go to sleep couched under their shields. I do not deny the presence of later strata in Homer. The rhapsodists could and did invent, as for that matter did the *fili*, and in making betrayed evidence of later conditions, e.g. cremation, but it seems they must also have preserved. Where we have preservation we have also a class charged with the duty. Only the trained memory can retain a richly developed and composite account, consistent as a story in itself and with itself. We know well the kind of thing preserved by unregulated popular memory, in the possession of everybody and anybody, the sport of vagrant fancy, brief and fugitive.

In Germanic antiquity dissimilar conditions prevailed. There is nothing which by any stretch of imagination can be regarded as a survival of the migration period, not to speak of earlier times. The Germans of Tacitus' day, or a little before, had epic lays of *Mannus* and the origin of the peoples ; later they had epic lays of Arminius. They have perished irretrievably, without a trace, and while the loss may be accident, not so the lack of trace. They were speedily antiquated and forgotten. It is the same with those of migration times ; they were transformed and supplanted. Gregory of Tours knows nothing of the Merovingians beyond Chlodvech's father, and as his knowledge plainly comes from a poem, it was the oldest he knew. If there were Anglo-Saxon lays about the conquest of England we know nothing of them. In Bede there are traces of lays, but all seventh-century ; in the Anglo-

Saxon Chronicle nothing clearly recognizable except a lay about Cynewulf in the eighth.[1] Alfred knew Anglo-Saxon poetry, but he did not supplement Bede for the early history of England, not because he would have disbelieved, nor yet that men did not make poems in Wessex. For the habits of the Anglo-Saxon *scop* we should compare *Beowulf* itself. The panegyric on *Beowulf* after the slaying of Grendel was a new poem. It included accounts of Sigemund and Heremod, who were certainly accounted of an earlier generation, but they were set side by side with Beowulf in a manner conditioned by the time of composition. Some of the difficulty of reconciling the *Finnsburh* fragment with the episode in *Beowulf* is that we have in each an independent treatment, and that in the episode the emphasis is laid elsewhere than in the lay. Why should they agree in detail? In Germanic poetry there is no approach to a canonical text, handed down by oral tradition for centuries, and if subject to alteration only so in a limited degree. A knowledge spread over a multitude of professional reciters, even if also makers, acts as a mutual corrective. In *Beowulf* we have not even a poem which was a national possession. It is well to dismiss accordingly any analogy with Homer. *Beowulf* occupied no such central position in Anglo-Saxon literature as Homer did in Greek. There is no demonstrable reference to it in the literature of the period, early or late, and if it had been so it could not have escaped notice. It was one among many, and its preservation is a sort of accident. Among the Anglo-Saxons there was no school of professional reciters, and if there had been, it is not *Beowulf* they would have preserved. The *scop* did not memorize the work of predecessors, he made the material anew. No doubt he borrowed new motives, new turns invented by others, approved and successful, hints in regard to dramatic situations and tragic emphasis, and he had at command

[1] *s.a.* 755.

a manner and an instrument, the common possession of all, beaten out through the generations, but he was first and last a maker. If we are to compare his situation with anything Greek, then it must be with the development of the mythus before Homer, and of that we know and probably can know nothing. I am protesting against the view that *Beowulf* carries us directly to the Germanic pagan past, and I shall endeavour to show that little or no trustworthy evidence of life and manners in the migration period, as distinct from later times, can be derived from the poem. Something certainly it owes to tradition, but when we ask for positive detail, the familiar touch of personal knowledge is absent ; we find only hints and suggestions, and these not seldom misunderstood. I should add that the accuracy of the historical detail embedded in the poem is a separate problem.

It has been asserted that, despite a Christian colouring, everything referred to in *Beowulf* is pagan. It is an exaggeration, even if the meaning is that everything is in origin of the pagan period. There are, however, rites and practices alluded to or described which cannot have been contemporary with Christianity, and it is well to examine these first to ascertain whether they lack precisely the sort of detail, the intimate familiarity in statement and silence we expect and get in normal descriptions of ordinary life. We have a ship-burial, two cremations, allusions to heathen rites and sacrifice and to auguries, possibly an oblique reference to the devotion of captive enemies to the heathen gods. The idea that the dragon's treasure is combined with a divergent account of a collection of arms devoted to the gods, and left *in situ*, cannot be sustained from the poem. Of those named the habit of augury could have survived though modified ; anyway, it is the merest allusion in a conventional phrase. Heathen rites and possibly sacrifice could be known at all events by hearsay. Sussex was heathen till 680, and if we may judge from Eddius, heathenism was in full force there. In Northumbria itself it lingered fairly late among outlying people in remoter parts, and it was to just such practices that not infrequent relapses during famine or pestilence tempted a sorely tried people. It matters little, for it is but an obscure and passing reference. The poet may, indeed must, have known more, but his silence is part of a deliberate policy of suppression of all that is shocking to Christian sentiment, and includes the details of Hrothwulf's birth and the exact relationship between Fitela and Sigemund. In those two instances we get nowhere. Besides, there is nothing really foreign to seventh-century England in either.

In the ship-burial and cremations it is not likely, in the former impossible, that the poet had personal knowledge or direct information. He was no doubt dependent on traditional accounts handed down in earlier lays. In the former we get no significant detail except that Scyld was placed by the mast—*mærne be mæste*—and a standard set up over him, and it may not be without importance that the characteristically Anglo-Saxon *segn* is employed. The jewels are to be expected, and ' from far lands ' is a traditional phrase suitable enough for any time. We have swords and corselets—our poet is fond of corselets—but no shields, though they are what we should look for. It may be part of the policy of suppression that there is no mention of horse, hawk, or hound, of wife or slaves, male or female. There is no mention of firing the vessel. Everything is general without a single point which must come from personal knowledge. There are also obscurities in the account, such as the word *īsig*, ' icy ', which may have had a meaning in the source but is dark to us, and here it should be observed that there are obscurities and textual difficulties in all the descriptions we have to consider. Some conceive the ship-burial as being carried out

without firing, and that is clearly the poet's belief. It is
evident from the nature of things that it cannot be shown
that it was not so, but our other descriptions include
firing, and I doubt if a different method would be employed
when the practice was alive. Ship-burial was practised
from Scandinavia to Japan, and a sixteenth-century
account from the latter throws an interesting light on
the attitude to the ship and its occupant.[1] There, like
Haki in *Ynglingasaga*,[2] the men were not yet dead, but
precautions had been taken, the men weighted with
stones and the ship stove in, while friends followed on
another and fired it. Any ship which is simply pushed
out to sea is the sport of wind and tide, the chances of its
being cast up somewhere are considerable, and not least
in the narrow seas of the Baltic. In the sixth century and
earlier men were not so naïve as to disregard the proximate
possibility of the treasure falling into other hands, of the
chance of dishonour to the dead, or what was worse, his
return, and they would have ensured his reaching the
desired destination in the only way they could. That is
conjecture. There remains the question of the mast,
which comes in twice, supporting the body, and carrying
the golden standard ' high over his head '. Among the
northern Teutons masts seem to have come late. Classical
writers of the fourth century speak of vessels which appear
to resemble coracles, and though it may be, it need not
be, an exaggeration. At all events, in Scandinavia by the
end of the third century we find at Nydam a fine clinker-
built ship, but it is mastless. The splendid Gokstad ship
often used to illustrate *Beowulf* has a mast, but belongs
to the end of the ninth century and the others associated
are about the same date. The recently discovered Kval-
sund boat is also a fine model, and it represents the sixth
century more nearly. It too is without mast. In the

[1] Hakluyt, *Principal Navigations* (Glasgow 1903-5), VI. 344.
[2] c. 23 (in *Heimskringla*, ed. F. Jónsson, 1911, p. 18).

ship graves at Upsala Stjerna assumed a mast because of the inferred sitting posture,[1] but the cremation of the Russ chieftain, to which we shall come presently, teaches us that there were other means of securing that ; the body was propped up with cushions. It is hazardous to make assertions on matters of the kind, as a discovery at any moment may overturn them, nevertheless at present it is more probable that Scandinavian boats of the sixth century and earlier seventh depended mainly or entirely on oars. In *Beowulf* it is otherwise. Ships are everywhere conceived as propelled by sails, and such was the familiar practice of late seventh-century England, and it is doubtless a good deal earlier. The expression *mǣrne be mǣste* may be inherited, but not from continental sixth-century lays. The other references to ships look like the familiar terms of a seventh-century poet. The similitude *fugle gelīcost* is sometimes explained with reference to the shape of the prow, but its use in Bede's life of Cuthbert, where five ships swept out to sea are compared with five birds on the waves, proves it a familiar idea.[2] It ought not to be forgotten that ship-burial was obsolete long before the sixth century. The ancient founder of the race of Scyldings is buried in an obsolete way, and even the poet's source may not have been accurately informed ; yet so far as we get any significant detail it points away from the early and towards the later period.

The situation is different in the cremation scenes, and especially in that of Beowulf. On the burning of Hnæf we need not linger. The account is very succinct, and the only noteworthy touch—significant because casual and unexplained—is the phrase *ēame be eaxle*, if we may accept Holthausen's brilliant conjecture. Reference ought to be made to further textual difficulties like *icge*, which with other things in that baffling synopsis defies explanation.

[1] *Op. cit.* p. 128.
[2] c. 3, in Complete Works (ed. J. A. Giles, 1843–4), IV. 216.

BEOWULF AND THE SEVENTH CENTURY

For *Beowulf*, on the other hand, we have a circumstantial account with precise detail. The resemblance with the burial of Attila, though there is no cremation there, has often been noted.[1] It is more singular that it has to my mind a closer resemblance with the practices as detailed in Homer, especially in *Odyssey* xxiv and *Iliad* xxiii, and even the Germanic and Greek terms for mounting the pyre coincide curiously—*bǣl āstīgan* and πυρῆς ἐπιβῆναι. There are several accounts of cremation in Scandinavian sources which have a general resemblance, and special attention should be called to the detailed description of a ship-cremation of a Russ, i.e. a Scandinavian, chieftain on the Volga in 921,[2] though the resemblance is not close, and it may have Scythian traits like those described in Herodotus iv. 71. A kind of suttee is practised, and a girl strangled and stabbed before the pyre is lighted. Boniface informs us that among the Wends suttee was practised in the eighth century,[3] and the Scandinavians knew it as late. In Homer we have the same account of the gathering of wood, the building of the pyre, the setting thereon of the dead, the firing of the pile, lamentation, gathering the bones, building on a sea-promontory of a mound to be seen by seafarers, living and to come. There are also sacrifice, the processional march round the pyre, weeping and lamentation followed by games. No urn is mentioned in *Beowulf*, but that can be paralleled from the Swedish burial-mounds. There the twelve chosen warriors circle the barrow, not the pyre as in Homer, or bier as in Jordanes,

[1] Jordanes, *De origine actibusque Getarum* c. 49 (ed. A. Holder, 1882), pp. 58–9.

[2] The most recent and complete version of this important notice is by C. Waddy in *Antiquity* viii (1934), 59 ff., where the author, usually cited as Ibn Fadhlan or Foszlan, is given as Ahmad bin Fudhlan. Besides the older versions of Dr. J. Anderson, there are others by Shetelig (from Montelius) in *Saga Book of the Viking Club* (1906) and by A. F. Major (following Shetelig) in *Folk-Lore* xxxv.

[3] Printed in W. de G. Birch, *Cart. Sax.* no. 172.

and it is there too the song in lament and honour is sung.
The parallel is extraordinarily close, and when we compare all the accounts with *Beowulf* we need not doubt that
it is in general accurate. It cannot be a contemporary
picture if my view of the poem is correct ; it must be con-
structed from the memory of earlier lays, and not necessarily lays about *Beowulf* or him alone. The general
accuracy can be due to the poet's nearness to the time
when the practice was alive, but we must consider whether
it is possible to detect anything which betrays ignorance
or misconception. I need not emphasize again the absence
of sacrifice, or difficulties in the text where *weaxan wonna
lēg* remains obscure in spite of all attempts to amend or
explain. There are besides some curious features, for
example, *windblond gelæg*, ' the wind ' or more precisely
' the tumult of winds was still ', the exact opposite of what
we should expect, or alternatively given in the wrong
place. In Homer the winds are summoned to the pyre,
in the Volga cremation a bystander remarks ' out of love
for him his lord has sent the wind to take him away this
very hour ', and even in Hnæf's the phrase, no doubt
traditional, *hlynode for hlǣwe*, ' roared in front of the
mound ', clearly suggests the action of wind. It would
seem that the poet has misunderstood his source. The
lack of precision with regard to *sēo gīomēowle* is suspicious
and suggests an original where all was clear as in Hnaef's
cremation, but most of all the hanging round of numerous
shields, corselets, and helmets is not paralleled. We might
pass the fact that they were hung, though it is strange,
but the evident suggestion of large numbers is more than
strange. That is perhaps what made Stjerna assume a
double account with two divergent conceptions of the
dragon's treasure.[1] It is more likely a simple mistake,
like the uncertainty in the statements about the disposal
of the hoard, but one no contemporary would make.

[1] *Op. cit.* pp. 136 ff.

Evidence for a double account can be obtained only by pressing the words unduly, and the notion that the dirge is given twice cannot be maintained. The lamentations of the woman and others at the burning is not on all fours with the solemn and ceremonial lament and encomium of the chosen retainers, the *lectissimi equites* of Jordanes. Plundering of grave-mounds was known in Anglo-Saxon times.[1] The arms and equipment would be as described *ōmige*, *þurhetone*, but the treasure would be intact. It is probable that traditional poetry preserved recollection of richer treasure in gold (such as occurs in Geatic territory) than was ever found in England; at the same time the conception of an immense treasure is in line with the general exaggeration of the poet. He insists, however, too strongly that the whole treasure is to accompany Beowulf and was buried in the barrow to make it a probable view that the armour burned with the body was part of the hoard. It must be equated rather with the armour and equipment which surrounded Scyld. We may guess that he had in mind something like the row of shields along the side of the vessel in a ship-burial, and associated the other weapons with the shields in ignorance of their purpose. However that may be, we are entitled to have doubts of our author's acquaintance with the rites he describes. There is nothing which could not come from tradition, and there are elements which excite misgiving.

We have finished with that which cannot be contemporary. For the rest I believe the poet is describing things, practices, and habits familiar in his day. Some of them could be survivals, particularly details of equipment and arms, and it is well to distinguish here between conventional epithets or phrases inherited by tradition and real description which proves knowledge. The damascened swords, no longer made, could have survived in use, though

[1] *Das angels. Prosa-Leben des hl. Guthlac*, ed. P. Gonser (Anglist. Forschungen 27), p. 117 (*Vita*).

38

some of the epithets, *ātertānum fāh, brogden-, sceāden-, wunden-mǣl* have the appearance of traditional expressions. We may be sure that *bunden golde* was not so, and if *fetel-hilt* means ' ringed hilt ' and is equivalent to *hring-mǣl*, it is worth recalling that Baldwin Brown believed the ring-hilted sword was an English invention because there we find a movable ring, elsewhere only a useless ornament.[1] We have one description of a sword, more precisely of a sword-hilt. Golden, it has serpentine devices and a runic inscription, apparently a poem. Runes on a sword-hilt need not surprise us, and their extent is a sort of poetic licence. The hilt is said to be *wreoþen*, and the word could mean ' twisted ', but that is not probable, nor is it likely that it means ' bound ', for binding was not usual, though one example does occur later, bound with silver wire. Rather it is employed in the same sense as *bunden-, wunden-* in combination with *stefna*, in reference to the twisted or coiled ornament on a ship's prow. This is supported by the association with *wyrmfāh*. Cassiodorus speaks of vermicular patterns on swords,[2] but we are concerned here not with a blade but with a hilt, and that is made so plain that it is not permissible to assume a conventional term misapplied. We must understand accordingly a design of serpents represented in spiral on the hilt, and thus on the grip, for the cross-pieces were occupied by the runes. It is a striking confirmation that we have just such ornament on a silver sword-hilt in the British Museum.[3] It is later, a full century later than the date suggested for the poem, but it seems to me, though I speak with hesitation on archaeological matters, that it is a developed specimen of a known type. Is it hazardous to suggest that the poet was describing a real sword ? The spiral ornament has its source in Celtic art with which

---

[1] *The Arts in Early England* III. 221 ff.
[2] *Variæ* v. 1 in *M.G.H. Auct. Ant.* XII. 143.
[3] Figured in *Vict. County Hist., London* I, plate facing p. 158.

Northumbria had close connexions, and there need be no doubt it was a native product.

The typical helmet in *Beowulf* is the mask-helmet (*grīma*) with nose-, cheek- and chin-guard, and boar-crest. The word was known later in that sense, and the helmet is described as by one familiar with it. Here we are on sound ground, for such helmets with animal crests complete are figured on the Franks Casket, and the Benty Grange helmet has nose-guard and boar-image. The corselet of chain is in part denoted by conventional epithets, and must in any case have been a survival, and at all times as scarce as it was costly. It is possible they too appear on the Franks Casket. They are believed to be of Roman provincial manufacture, and that may be taken as certain, for they were known in Britain during the late Roman period, as is proved by the fragments found in Carling-wark Loch, Kirkcudbright, and elsewhere.[1] These have the same arrangement of welded and riveted rings as the Scandinavian finds, and all are a good deal earlier than the poem. None has been dug up in Scandinavia in the migration or Viking period, though references in Scandinavian literature are frequent. It would seem that the poet's knowledge need not have come from thence. Of other weapons or equipment nothing need be said. Shield and spear, short sword, bow and arrows, and with them horn or trumpet—they are proper to any period. The *realien*, including others to come, are contemporary with the poet.

The society, as in all heroic poetry, is aristocratic ; there is no attempt to envisage a whole people. Even within its limits the picture is fragmentary, and we have but a partial account of matters connected with warfare, the business and occupation of king and retinue. There is

[1] *Proc. Soc. Ant. Scot.* (1931–2), p. 321.

no description of their habitual acts and employment. Except incidentally there is no reference to hunting, riding in contest, amusements and the like ; the ordinary facts of life are taken for granted, likewise the familiar surroundings. The hall is not described nor its contents. Feasting is mentioned, but we have no details of a feast, and food is not mentioned, so unlike Homer, except in the most general terms. Drinks, especially wine, are just named, and wine was common enough in seventh-century England, known but hardly common in sixth-century Scandinavia. The vessels too are named only in a general way, *sincfæt, sele-ful, wunderfatu*. Richly ornamented and costly bowls were certainly known, but the commoner sort of dish does not come in at all ; nor does silver or glass, though a costly Anglo-Saxon goblet of glass was made, valued, and exported. Everything specifically indicated is gold. This may be a traditional trait, or part of an atmosphere of exaggeration ; at all events the profusion of gold must be explained on some such lines. Tapestries are mentioned, but as something strange and unusual, and this accords well with the introduction of painted and embroidered cloths for religious purposes in the seventh century ; later they were common and would not excite remark. The retainers sleep in the hall, but we get no indication of the type of beds. They may have been on a raised platform running along the side, and used as a bench in daytime, but that is not certain. What is clear is that tables and perhaps benches were removed when the hall was prepared for night, and the arms placed above the sleeping men. The custom corresponds with that in use in England. The character and construction of the hall also corresponds. The chief building in a court surrounded with ditch and rampart, it was rectangular, with two doors opening on the court, one in each of the narrower sides, and seats along the longer walls. These details can be established from English accounts, and we have on the

Franks Casket a plan with high-seat indicated. Beowulf
enters by one door, and advancing takes his stand in front
of the king and on the hearth (adopting a probable emenda-
tion), and later is disposed in a seat of honour opposite.
The king had besides his private apartments, and that
is naturally Germanic as well as English, but in the very
considerable court pictured in the poem there were numerous other houses for the accommodation of the king's
attendants and guests, which is more in line with English
conditions. On the second night of his stay Beowulf and
his band were accommodated apart ; and this implies no
inconsiderable establishment. I may refer also to Wealhtheow's group of attendant women. Moreover, the poet
seems to have had an actual city in mind, if we may make
an inference from his use of *ceaster* and from other indications. Both *burg* and *ceaster* were familiar, but an
apparent variation in the account may be a conflict of
traditional with contemporary conditions. Without doubt
some of the Roman towns of northern England, notably
York, were occupied by the Anglo-Saxons, and the picture
of Hrothgar's court suggests unmistakably a considerable
settlement and population. We learn, though we get no
details, of people who were responsible for the setting in
order of the hall, the service of guests and others, the care
of the king's horse. Some may have been noble, as he
who acted as a kind of chamberlain certainly was, and
the *ðyle*, whose position and duties are obscure. He sat
at the lord's feet, and in later Anglo-Saxon times we have
the *pedisessor*, *pedisecus*, one of whom was of the highest
rank. The term is significant not only of the kind of
nobility but of kingship, but to that we shall return
presently.

The society described is not only aristocratic and military,
it is on a permanent war-footing. There is a suggestion
of officials and councillors, but the fighting force fills the

42

picture, and that recruited from the nobility. Other classes hardly exist. A slave is introduced. His status is certain, for he had fled from scourging, and that was the punishment of a slave (flogging a freeman implied loss of status), and the mention is contemptuous. The freeman does not appear unless the *ceorl* introduced in a simile is intended as one.[1] If so, and it may be doubted, the poet at once forgets his status and passes into a typical description of the deserted hall and empty chamber of a young noble. A story in Bede makes it apparent that there was a sharp distinction between noble and peasant, for a young man is recognized as noble by his face, demeanour, and discourse.[2] Whatever may have been true earlier, the effective fighting force in seventh-century England was the personal retinue, and it is not clear there was any other. It is said of Hrothgar that he was successful in war and so (it is to be understood) his retinue increased. That was the situation in England. To be powerful or to maintain independence a strong retinue was necessary. With such Ceadwalla was able to make himself master for a time in Sussex, and later established himself in Wessex. We are told of Oswini attracting to his service men from all quarters, even the most noble.[3] We learn too that irresponsible bands existed at that time. Guthlac had no rule anywhere, but he was lord of a retinue, and his actions in regard to the conquests he made, the tribute he exacted, and the booty he won, were quite independent.[4] His is not the only case in point.

The personal retinue is common Germanic. It had its origin in the family group, as some of its names, though long conventional, bear witness—*magodriht, sibbegedriht, winemāgas*. We know from Tacitus that the *Germani* fought in family groups, but already in his day the retinue

---

[1] ll. 2444 ff.   [2] *Hist. Eccl.* IV. xxii.   [3] *Ibid.* III. xiv.
[4] *Vita S. Guthlaci* c. 10 (ed. P. Gonser, *ut supra*, pp. 108–9).

in its later form existed, and nobles thought it no disgrace to be in such service. The altered constitution appears in such names as *gestas* (for that is what *gest* means in Wihtræd's laws)[1] and in our poem *fēðegestas*, though this name too has become conventional. The *wrecca* or warrior exiled by choice or necessity from his homeland is a characteristic figure ; the hostage during his stay at a prince's court was in all respects like other members. The oath which Ecgtheow swore to Hrothgar and the mutual oaths of Finn and Hengest reflect the relation between Penda and Eadfrith. It is not conceivable that a man even of princely rank could make a lengthy sojourn at the court of another without entering into the relation of virtual retainer. The Teutons were generous in the reception of strangers, but the period of stay was limited to three days, and it is perhaps not an accident that three nights was the duration of Beowulf's stay at Heorot. It is clear that every feature we can trace is in accord with English practice.

A few points may be emphasized. The relation was voluntary in both sides and terminable by either. No doubt many entered for life, mostly those drawn from the king's own people, but the fact that the retinue was recruited from far afield, and that foreign princes could be members temporarily, involves the habit of withdrawal, and we know of such cases. I think it probable that young princes were in the habit of winning their spurs at the court of another. Paulus Diaconus has a story of one getting arms from another king,[2] and I should like to associate it with the case of Heoroweard in *Beowulf*.[3] Oswald's son and two sons of Oswiu were at different times in Penda's retinue, and we should remember what Beowulf says of the young Hrethric. How else could he

---

[1] § 20, in F. Liebermann, *Die Gesetze der Angelsachsen* (1903–6), I. 14.

[2] *Pauli historia Langobardorum*, ed. L. Bethman and G. Waitz (Mon. Germ. Hist., 1878), p. 61.　　　　[3] ll. 2160 ff.

visit foreign courts except in such a capacity ? Again it was a personal relation. This also applied mutually, but is chiefly important on the side of the retainer. On the king's death the retinue did not pass as a matter of course to his successor ; a new bond had to be made. It is obvious, for the kingship itself did not pass as a matter of course. Those who argue that Hengest cannot have been of royal rank, because after Hnæf's death his men were lordless, mistake the situation. Hæthcyn's men were equally lordless after Ravenswood,[1] though Hygelac his brother succeeded to the kingdom and no doubt took over the survivors. There are other points to be regarded, but so far as concerns the retinue, it is possible that Hengest was brother or son of Hnæf. It was not a matter which went without saying that the son should have the support of his father's following, as the remark on Scyld's son at the beginning of the poem makes plain. In the third place, while it lasted the bond overrode all other claims whatever—kindred, patriotism, and what not. This accounts for the unmeasured condemnation everywhere expressed for betrayal of the lord, for the fact that we often find men in arms against what we should call king and country. It accounts too for one of the favourite tragic motives in Germanic literature, the rival claims of kindred and loyalty, and thereby the meeting of kindred, such as father and son, in hostile encounter. It explains finally the sacrifice of life and liberty in defence of the lord. As is well known, the last is glorified in poetry and presented as an ideal of true service as a retainer. Examples need not be adduced, but we should beware of regarding the complete destruction of the retinue as the inevitable concomitant of the lord's fall, at least in cases where he was a national king and a duty lay on the nobility of preserving national existence. It should be added that in early times, and especially in northern Europe, the body cannot

[1] *hláfordléase*, l. 2935.

have been really large. Ammianus Marcellinus tells of one numbering two hundred and more,[1] but that would be exceptional for the North. The considerable size of the retinue which may be inferred in *Beowulf* is an indication of English conditions. The Anglo-Saxon states acquired prominence in proportion to their opportunities of warlike employment. The early decline of Kent and Sussex is so explained ; their opportunities of booty were restricted. Northumbria flourished while it was the fighting front of Anglo-Saxon aggression. Mercia, which had equal chances, later took its place, and Wessex was important for the same reason, but lagged behind because less unified, and afflicted by frequent internecine strife. In conclusion, the picture of the retinue is that of a body familiar in every detail to the Anglo-Saxon, Germanic undoubtedly, but only so to the extent and with the modifications with which it survived in England. It was so much a part of the common order that it passed into religion, in literature and in life, and followers were regarded, and regarded themselves, as the bodyguard of their leader, to live with him and die with and for him.

The same claim must be made for the institution of kingship as described in *Beowulf*. It used to be said that the conquest developed the king, and it is probably true that it developed the kind we know in England, nor is it unlikely that added to the influence of the conquest was that of Roman organization even in its extreme decrepitude. Kings go back as far as we can trace historically and beyond, attached to them was an aura of sanctity in virtue of their divine descent, perhaps an echo of the time when they were priest-kings, but there is no evidence of an organized authority. We should hold apart the peoples who came into contact with Roman civilization. Turning attention to the Scandinavian lands, we find there a primitive atmosphere in sharp contrast with the dignity and

[1] Ammianus Marcell. (Bk. XVI, cap. 12, § 60), *ed. cit.* I. p. 101.

aloofness of kingship in the poem. The difference is as apparent in Saxo as in the sagas. There is the story of Frotho in Saxo, advised by his retinue to get him a wife because of the sorry plight of their clothing which needed a woman to mend them.[1] We appreciate the difference if we compare the coming of Beowulf to Hrothgar with coast-warden and elaborate etiquette, or Beowulf's return home with ceremonial entry after reception by the harbour-warden, with Bothvar Bjarki's arrival at the court of Hrolf, with Egil's meeting with Eirik at York, or with Authun and his white bear seeking the king. The *hȳðweard* is the mark of a community organized for trade and revenue, as the *ǣgweard* of one organized for defence. We know there was a considerable settlement of Frisians in York for trading purposes in the eighth century,[2] and it is likely they were there already in the seventh; there was at all events a lively intercourse between Northumbria and the Continent. When we remember also the grant of a principality to Beowulf with official sword and a territory of seven thousand hides, we inevitably think of English conditions. The atmosphere is throughout that of a large and powerful court, with its officials on duty at home, and others discharging important functions abroad, that is to say, an organized state. It is impossible to avoid the conclusion that the poet is describing the conditions round him.

The point comes out in other ways, for example in the attitude to the succession. There is the evident suggestion that Hrethric had a right to succeed his father, and Heardred his; in early times they had at most a right to be considered. In England the old view survived long, but in Northumbria by the seventh century it seems clear that the right of son to succeed father had established itself.

[1] *Saxonis Grammatici Gesta Danorum*, ed. A. Holder (1886), p. 122.
[2] *Vita S. Ludgeri* i. 10 in *Acta Sanctorum* (Boll.) Martii III. 643, col. 1.

That conception dominates the poem and determines Beowulf's action with regard to his cousin. He seems to have exercised a sort of regency, much as may have been done in Mercia by the nobles under Wulfhere.[1] Such a position is not credible for the early sixth century. The first thought of the regent would be to get rid of inconvenient claimants as Hrothwulf did, and as was done in Kent by Ecgberht at a date perhaps a little earlier than our poem, and I dare say the knowledge of it explains in some measure the horror and condemnation with which the poet views Hrothwulf. It is not the only pointed parallel we can draw from contemporary history. Oswiu was as unfortunate in the marriage alliances of his daughters as a means of patching up peace with the Mercians as Hrothgar with the Heathobeards. In both cases strife broke out anew, accompanied by death of kindred. Such things can naturally be paralleled outside England, but it is noteworthy that two should occur within a brief compass. The disastrous results of strife within the family or marriage connexion evidently oppressed the poet. He returns to it again in the Finnsburh story, a story certainly told *à propos*, following immediately on the entry of Hrothgar and Hrothwulf and the statement that as yet their friendship endured. Hrothgar's reference to the king who suffered from $ὕβρις$ is not impossibly an oblique allusion to Ecgfrith and the disaster in which he was involved. I could add many traits in *Beowulf* which are definitely English, like the *fāgan flōr* which is too familiar a descriptive term to admit any but the usual sense of ' tessellated pavement ', or else Germanic traits in full life in England, but I have said enough to substantiate the claim that in *Beowulf* we move in surroundings essentially Anglo-Saxon.

What is true of physical and material things is no less true in the intellectual and moral sphere. Something has

[1] Bede, *Hist. Eccl.* III. xxiv.

48

been indicated incidentally. That the new conditions were largely due to Christianity is obvious. Chivalrous actions can be cited from earlier times, but it is not a question of isolated acts of kindness and chivalry, but of mental attitude, and a decisive change can easily be proved. In England there was plenty of the older behaviour, dynastic quarrels and murder of kindred, violence, treachery, aggression, lust and crime, but it provoked condemnation, if not abnormal it contradicted the better way known and approved. It is clear that the public conscience was shocked by Ecgfrith's unprovoked attack on Ireland, and by his ὕβρις in general, by Ecgberht of Kent, by the wife of Peada, by the murder of Oswini, and the behaviour of Eadbald, and the poem is in line with the newer sentiment or even more advanced. The hero is presented as an ideal king or warrior, and his every act, except the Breca episode, is designed to be and described as helpful and generous, while the swimming match at least can excite no reprobation. All action contrary to the ideal is condemned explicitly, or implicitly—Heremod, Unferth, Thryth and others. The evil which issues from dynastic strife, from blood and violence, is emphasized. This ameliorating influence is clearly earlier than the formal acceptance of Christianity. Edwin was predisposed to the new religion before his conversion, the result, it may be, of his sojourn among Britons. It is certain at all events that in Northumbria the old religion had lost much of its hold among the nobility and in court circles, and the words of the councillor and the high-priest, which Bede recites in his story of Edwin's conversion, show how weak was the opposition Christianity had to meet.[1] In line are the marriages of Christian princesses with leave to practise their religion, the attitude of Penda to the new faith, the settlement of Christian hermits in various parts, the absence of martyrs, and the apparent readiness with

[1] *Hist. Eccl.* II. xiii.

which Christian missionaries were everywhere received and settled without interference. Only in London do we hear of a persistent opposition, and the position and population there were exceptional.

One characteristic of *Beowulf* which cannot easily be separated from the English environment, and at that precise time, is the atmosphere of pensive melancholy, a mood of sorrow excited by the decay of the splendours of the past, by the destruction which attends mortality and the works of man. Nowhere in England more than in Northumbria were men in the presence of an imposing greatness which had passed away. The ground was littered with the ruined fragments of a past which impressed the imagination as vividly as it provoked curiosity, but was only imperfectly understood, and remained mysterious, menacing—*eald enta geweorc.* Deserted chambers rich in decoration, the empty temples of forgotten gods called forth an emotional response issuing in a sense of the transience of man's life and works, which in poetry expressed itself in a melancholy characteristic of all Anglo-Saxon verse, and in life translated itself into a desire for escape from the burden of the world, an other-worldliness notable in Northumbria and not there alone. Secular duties were neglected and men and women crowded into monasteries, the kings not seldom leading the way. The words of Bede are apposite ; ' such being the peaceable and calm disposition of the times many of the Northumbrians, as well of the nobility as of private persons, laying aside their weapons rather incline to dedicate themselves and their children to the tonsure and monastic vows than to study martial discipline '.[1] In Ceolfrith's time there were near seven hundred monks in Wearmouth-Jarrow, and the number of men devoted to a monastic life must have been a high proportion of the population. North-

[1] *Hist. Eccl.* V. xxiii.

umbria's decline is not hard to understand. This emotional —even sentimental—attitude to life suits the later seventh century and no earlier time. In the poem its influence is everywhere, not only expressly as in Hrothgar's long speech with his sorrow over his lost youth (though that point can be paralleled in early days), in the words of the last survivor, in Hrethel's attitude as interpreted by the poet, implicitly in Beowulf's words to Wiglaf when dying and in his account of his early life. We have battle, death and fate, but no ' delight of battle '. There is more of that in the few lines of *Finnsburh* than in all *Beowulf*.

> Over the slain the dusky raven flew
> Black, while the unceasing flicker of steel on steel
> Made all Finn's castle seem one blaze of flame.

Combat and vengeance for kindred is a grave and sombre duty which must be faced in the sober spirit in which Beowulf goes out to meet the dragon ; the situation is ominous. The ultimate approval is not for the successful captain but for him who had secured for his people a long reign of peace, like Hrothgar, Beowulf ; and again let us remember that Beowulf's acts are all glorified as acts meant to check and destroy those who menace men's peaceful existence.

I have tried to show a close correspondence between seventh-century conditions in Northumbria and the poem both in the material and intellectual side. It should not be forgotten that we know more of Northumbria just then than of any other part of England, but I think we know enough to confirm belief that the correspondence is closer than elsewhere.

There remains a last question touching the people themselves. The character of the population of Northumbria is a difficult problem, and the history of the English settle-

ment there is obscure. Bede knows nothing, and if there
were native traditions he is ignorant of them. The absence
of Anglo-Saxon burials and remains in south-eastern Scotland (i.e. in the northern part of Bernicia) is held to
justify the conclusion that it was settled and incorporated
late, not before the seventh century. That can be. There
is, however, a similar condition in southern Bernicia, the
modern Northumberland. Chadwick has suggested that
Bernicia was an offshoot from Deira,[1] while Thurlow Leeds
goes further and assumes a conquest by Ida about 550.[2]
In that case it is curious that the old tradition dates the
kingdom of Bernicia fourteen years earlier than Deira, and
it ought to be observed that Thurlow Leeds' view runs
counter to such early notices as we possess. He thinks
that Ida captured Bamborough about 550, on what
authority I do not know, unless it be an inference from
the fact that it has a Welsh name. Moreover, the theory
does not meet the difficulty, unless we are to assume that
there could be no pagan cemeteries between 550 and 626,
for Bernicia was certainly settled or anglicized very rapidly
if the process began in 550. Fifty years later Æthelfrith
defeated what is called an ' immense army ' led by Aidan
at Degsastan with the resources of Bernicia alone.[3] Immense may be an exaggeration, but a coalition of Scots
from Ireland and Scotland, Britons, perhaps Picts, and
apparently some dissident Angles, cannot have been inconsiderable. Though our accounts say that Bernicia was
hotly assailed during the preceding half-century and occasionally in difficulties, its resistance must have been effective, and it does not seem probable that there is time for
growth in power and numbers to meet such an attack.
There is no reason to believe there was any considerable
movement of population towards the close of the century,

[1] *Origin of the English Nation* (1912), p. 183.
[2] *Archaeology of the Anglo-Saxon Settlements* (1913), p. 72 f.
[3] Bede, *Hist. Eccl.* I. xxxiv.

or that there was any extensive colonization from abroad, yet Bede, writing of the activities of Paulinus in Bernicia, gives the impression of a considerable English population, and knows nothing of its being recently established. It may be accordingly that we should seek another explanation of the absence of Anglo-Saxon remains on both sides of the Border, namely, that the population, though anglicized in speech and in culture generally, was really mixed. In Deira, archaeological evidence of the Angles is abundant, but there too a variety of circumstances gives support to the view that numbers of the previous inhabitants were incorporated, and that the settlement throughout Northumbria is not on a par with that in East Anglia, Essex, Sussex, or even Wessex. The names *Beornice, Dere*, are unlike those employed elsewhere, not only *Eastseaxe*, but also *Cantware, Lindisfare*; they are the only examples of British names used simply. In the *Historia Brittonum* we are told that the district in the vicinity of the Roman Wall was granted to Octha and Ebissa,[1] just as Kent was granted to Hengest. Plummer discredited the story on the ground that the people would be Jutes,[2] but there may be a germ of truth in the grant, or possibly settlement with consent, though a son of Hengest may not come in. There are good grounds for doubting if the people in Kent were Jutes or all Jutes, and a Saxon aetiological myth is attached to the person of Hengest himself. It has been too readily assumed, moreover, that the enemies against whom Vortigern engaged mercenaries were Scots and Picts alone. Classical writers mention Saxons continually in association with them, and it is not credible that their attacks ceased because Vortigern called in a band of Jutes or others to his aid. That Gildas and other British authorities should get confused between the two groups of Teutons is not surprising, especially as it was inevitable

[1] c. 38.
[2] C. Plummer, *Two of the Saxon Chronicles Parallel*, II. 15 (*s.a.* 547).

that in time they should act in concert. Schütte suggested recently that in the North there remained considerable remnants of a population descended from the Teutonic forces on the Wall.[1] If there is any truth in his theory, the Celtic element must have been much modified, and amalgamation with Teutonic settlers facilitated. Conversely there would be a modification of Germanic rites and practices, and this may well have affected the disposal of the dead.

All this would be in line with the Roman influence traceable in Northumbria, e.g. the coinage from Rome through the Britons. Edwin is the only king of whom we read that he had an ensign carried before him, and it suggests a Roman reminiscence, a claim to authority over the whole Roman province. It has been maintained that the distribution of a man's property in thirds—one to the wife, one to the children, one in the disposal of the testator —is a survival of Roman law in London.[2] I do not know if any weight can be placed on that, but if so it is noteworthy that thus Dryhthelm in Northumbria disposed his property on retiring into Melrose, and Bede describes it in terms which indicate a recognized practice.[3] Altogether these points and other points support the belief of a mixed population in Northumbria.

In addition to this mixture the contact of Briton and Angle seems to have been more intimate in the sixth and seventh centuries than usually allowed. The impression of separation is due to an ecclesiastical animus, very evident in Bede, who is as a rule so honest and unbiased, and even in him it is more political than racial, that is, not directed against those Britons, and they were many, included in the Northumbrian kingdom of his day. The pretext for

[1] *Our Forefathers* II. 260 ff.   [2] E. Thurlow Leeds, *op. cit.* p. 53.
[3] *Hist Eccl.* V. xii.

the animus, whatever the cause, was the failure of missionary enterprise on the part of the Britons among the English. If a tithe of what Gildas says about the condition of Christianity is true, or if what we gather from the life of Kentigern represents the state among Britons, then it is not surprising that missionary activity failed. So far as we can see, the paganism of the invader was more active in attracting the native. There is plenty of evidence in Bede of English seeking refuge and sojourning among the British. Guthlac spoke Welsh.[1] Eddius makes it plain that in Deira Angle and Briton lived side by side, and amicably enough, and some of the famous names in Northumbrian story are in their origin British and suggest British blood. According to Nennius, Oswiu's first wife was a woman of that race, and the same authority states that Edwin was baptized by a British priest.[2] The statement has been rejected, but unless we are to reject the authority of the document entirely, and reasonable grounds adduced, there is nothing improbable in the fact. Paulinus was not Augustine, chiefly concerned with the assertion of ecclesiastical authority, and a tradition of activity among Britons suggests that he did not hold himself aloof.

I am suggesting that in Northumbria, varying in degree according to district, we have mixture of people and close contact. A good many years ago Stopford Brooke sought the explanation of the sudden outburst of literature, art, and scholarship in Northumbria in precisely this intermingling of blood.[3] That is a matter of subjective judgment, but it is a fact which demands some explanation that this blossoming of art should have occurred just then and there, and that the impulse to creative activity is not

---

[1] *Vita S. Guthlaci* c. 19 (ed. P. Gonser, *ut supra*, p. 136).

[2] Nennius, *Hist. Britt.* cc. 57, 63 (Mon. Germ. Hist. 1898, pp. 203, 206).

[3] *History of Early English Literature* (1892), c. xiv.

matched anywhere else or at any other time in Anglo-Saxon England. It is not impossible that we have therein a clue to some of its characteristics. The note of reflective melancholy we trace in *Beowulf* is not a new trait in Northumbrian poetry, for the unknown genius who, as the seventh century drew to its close, celebrated in a new spirit the glories of the old heroic life, picturing his ideal king with soul bucklered against the blows of fate, but with a persistent undertone of sadness over the transiency of human endeavour, regret for the things which have been but can never return, is the heir of the nameless poet who at Edwin's court expressed his sense of the futility of life, when darkened by ignorance and unillumined by hope.

III

FOLK-TALE AND HISTORY

THE subject of *Beowulf* is a conflict with two water-monsters who are in turn despatched, and after a long interval a conflict with a dragon laying waste the country-side. It too is killed by the hero who, however, gets his own death in the encounter. Both conflicts, for the first, though double, is to be regarded as one, are set amid an historical environment at a definite time, and real people are introduced in person or by allusion. There are numerous references to historical events or events which profess to be historical, but the history is the frame and the background, and the canvas is occupied by a couple of folk-tales seemingly as old as humanity. We need not doubt that such subjects were cultivated from the beginning by the Germanic poet, and it is certain that they lingered on in the people's memory. Tales of dragons together with a belief in dragons survived till recent times, and the popular mind is apt to accept with credulity stories of water-monsters. The stories, moreover, are often attached to real persons and localized precisely in time and place. The habit is so well known that examples are superfluous.

The two folk-tales in *Beowulf* have parallels elsewhere. Several more or less close can be adduced for the dragon-conflict. Of greater interest is the striking parallel with the earlier conflict found in the Icelandic *Grettissaga*. In it we have the identical story with a different hero and in

57

a different historical setting. There seems no doubt that the versions are independent, but that nevertheless the special form of the folk-tale is determined in both by a common source which cannot lie very far back. Differences in detail have developed, but these issue in part from the variant environment ; in part they are due to a definitely rationalizing tendency more advanced in the later account. Grettir is afraid of the dark, but in *Beowulf* we move in a pervading atmosphere of mystery and awe. The monsters are not only dangerous, they are portentous, and everything about them shares in and contributes to the sensation of terror. The sense of something uncanny is emotionally stressed by the poet. These beings are not only destructive and evil as in *Grettissaga*, they are allied to the powers of darkness which have their hour when sight fails, and the other senses are but so many avenues for intimations of the terrible. Their uncanny nature is apparent in the reference to the *helrūnan*, ' sorcerers ' or ' wizards of hell ', whose comings and goings no man knows, and it is emphasized in the description of the coming of Grendel to Heorot. Nowhere is it plainer than in the description of the haunted mere which is their dwelling, lonely, desolate, shunned by all living things but creatures of the deep, ringed with grey trees stark against the sky, and probably imagined by the poet as still with the silence of death.

The resemblances between *Beowulf* and *Grettissaga* have been set forth so often that there is no need to enlarge upon them. It is sufficient to point out that not only is the setting in *Grettissaga* historical, but the hero is also a real person. I mention it now because many doubt whether Beowulf was a real person, or rather it is commonly taken for granted that he was not. To that question I shall return in the sequel, but it is so intimately connected with the question of the general accuracy of the history that it claims attention first.

Before proceeding to the historical question there is another matter of moment on which it is proper to dwell briefly, a point involving the normal attitude of mind in *Beowulf* touching those things which transgress the limits of nature. I have spoken of a rationalizing tendency in *Grettissaga*, and we have, though in less measure, something similar in the poem. Someone has said that beast- and monster-stories take us back to the very heart of Germanic antiquity. They would if we could gather them in their primitive form, but in *Beowulf* we shall not find a primitive mentality, though the actual content may be unchanged. We have none of that attitude to the magical and supernatural which appears, for example, so strikingly in the Irish epic cycle *Táin Bó Cúalnge*. A changed outlook on life has left a deep impress on the folk-tale. Grendel and his dam may inherit cannabalistic features from the *eotonas* of old, but their position is explained and motivated in a manner to appeal to reason. Their outcast state has its root in descent from Cain, and the curse of Cain hangs heavy upon them. They are no longer embodied evil and destruction, motiveless malignity which men cannot explain, avoid, or appease. Everything about them has been reduced to the plane of reason and of experience, or at least all but one thing, that some of the limitations incident to humanity are removed, and the hero shares in part in the freedom from such limitations. We are, with few exceptions, in a world governed by the capacities and restrictions of human nature. To appreciate the distinction it is worth while to contrast Beowulf with the Irish hero Cuchulain in the *Táin Bó Cúalnge*. I will not dwell on the contrast, but I may take the opportunity to point out that the root of the *Táin* is history, if not a particular event, yet a generalization of something which happened repeatedly, and amidst this setting taken from normal experience is introduced in a manner to dominate the whole an enveloping atmosphere of marvel and magic utterly absent from our epic, based though it is on a primordial folk-tale. I need not refer to tabu, to super-natural creatures with more than human powers ; it is sufficient to refer to the hero Cuchulain himself. I put aside the three vats of cold water necessary to cool his wrath, of which, when he was set therein, the first burst its staves, the second boiled with bubbles as large as fists, and the third had a heat which possibly *some* men might endure, and with the vats also the marvellous barbed weapon, shot from the fork of the foot, which spread in the body of the victim and filled every joint and sinew with its barbs. It is enough to take one point where there is an express resemblance with Beowulf. Of him it is said that he overtaxed every sword with the strength of his hand and blow,[1] but Cuchulain when being fitted with arms by Conchobar shivers in turn by his brandishing some fourteen sets of spears, sword and shield before he is fitted with the king's own arms, and shivers into fragments an equal number of chariots before finding in the king's chariot one which will serve.[2] Exaggeration of that type and to that degree is alien from the spirit of *Beowulf* even where the subject might seem to invite it. It at least, and perhaps Germanic heroic poetry in general, has a firm hold on reality, on the facts of life as it is lived among men, and from its conduct of those events which lie beyond the boundary of the normal we derive a surer sense of confidence in everything which is set forth as history or as part of man's ordinary lot.

The history in *Beowulf* includes reference to kings who play a part in the poem, to their family relations and con-nexions, as well as to others appearing only in passing allusion. The former sort are named and set in mutual relation, among them kings of Danes, Heathobeards, Geats and Swedes. We have reference to or accounts of raids,

[1] ll. 2684 ff.   [2] E. Windisch, *Irische Texte*, IV. Suppl. pp. 132 ff.

war and conquest, for example, wars of Danes and Heathobeards, Geats and Swedes, but for the most part we cannot
test the truth of the narrative by trustworthy historical
evidence. In one case and one only we are more fortunately situated. On several occasions the poem mentions
a raid on the territory of a people variously described as
Frēsan, Frisians, *Hetware*, the classical Chattuarii, *Froncan*,
Franks, and *Hugas*, another name for the Franks. The
raid was made by Hygelac, king of the Geats, who is an
important figure in the poem, and it ended disastrously
for him in defeat and death. The identical raid is described or alluded to in three Frankish sources, in
Gregory of Tours,[1] who wrote fifty or sixty years after
the event, in a *Liber Historiae Francorum* of the beginning of the eighth century,[2] and in a possibly earlier
Liber Monstrorum de Diversis Generibus.[3] The two former
designate the raiders Danes, but the last preserves a more
accurate recollection of the people, though they are mis-
called *Getae* instead of *Gauti*. Combining the accounts,
we arrive at the following synopsis. A king of the Geats
named Chochilaicus made an attack on the territory of
the Frankish king. He came by sea with a fleet and
wasted certain districts round the mouth of the Rhine,
among others that occupied by the *Attoarii*, and loaded
his ships with captives and booty. While the ships were
making their way to the open sea the king remained on
shore on an island. He and they were attacked by a
powerful force despatched by the king of the Franks and
defeated with great slaughter. The king of the Geats was
killed, his corpse remaining in the possession of the enemy,
and the booty was recaptured and restored.

There is no detail of this account and very certainly no
vital detail which does not appear in the poem either in
direct statement or inferentially. The name *Attoarii* is

---

[1] *Hist. Franc.* iii. 3. For editions of this and the two works next
referred to, see R. W. Chambers, *Beowulf : an Introduction*, pp. 3-4.
[2] c. xix.   [3] i. 3.

identical with *Hetware* and *Chochilaicus* is an earlier and
Frankish form of *Hygelac*. Theudoric and Theudobert his
son, who was in command of the Franks, are not mentioned by name, but the Franks are named as such and
as *Hugas*, and the dynastic name Merovingian occurs.
The peoples involved determine the district as the Rhine.
It is not said definitely that it was a raid for booty, nor
that the king was on shore or on an island, but booty was
the obvious purpose, and an island is probable, for it is
clear that the king was on shore. He was attacked and
killed under arms, his corpse is said to have remained in
the enemy's possession, and Beowulf had to swim off.
It is evident too from the narrative that Beowulf's exploits,
killing his king's slayer and fighting his way out, were on
land. The strong force of the Frankish historians becomes
in the poem a superior force (*mid ofermægene*), and the
recapture of the booty is not only obvious from the result
of the engagement but inferentially stated in the absence
of reward for the Geats. The poet refers to the expedition
in four different places, and there are discrepancies in his
account, but the motive for these is understandable. In
one of the later references he minimizes the losses, in
another he exalts the prowess of Beowulf. He says
(ll. 2501 ff.) that the king's ornaments did not fall into
the enemy hands, but he has stated previously (ll. 1203 ff.)
that the most notable ornament did come into the possession of the enemy, and with it armour and corpse. It is
possible that the later reference may be or may originally
have been personal to Dæghrefn, that he, the slayer of
Hygelac, did not live to take the ornaments to his king.
The poet states also (ll. 2334 ff.) that Beowulf bore off
with him thirty suits of armour from the enemy. This
need not be taken too literally. The underlying meaning
is clear, namely, that he accounted for a fair number of
Franks, and the taking of the armour is typical, the normal
result of success. The enemy warrior Dæghrefn, whose

name is apparently Frankish and possibly authentic, is spoken of as carrying the spoils to the Frisian king, *Frēscyninge*. That can mean Theudoric or his deputy, for Theudobert is also entitled to the designation *cyning*. They were kings of all the peoples over whom they ruled, and just before the poet has characterized Dæghrefn as *Huga cempa*, that is, warrior or champion of the Franks. There is a complete, even a surprising agreement in the accounts, surprising when we consider that one of the versions has come down in the form of historic lay. I have dwelt on the agreement down to small details because this one historical event which we can check by early authoritative testimony gives proof of the high degree of accuracy we may fairly expect in the history embedded in *Beowulf*. When it is history in the strict sense it can be trusted as sound.

In all other cases we have to depend on internal tests, the inner consistency of the narrative, or else on evidence derived from Scandinavian tradition. It should be said at once that on all points which it touches our poem is by far the oldest evidence we possess and, with an isolated exception, certainly the best. The Scandinavian accounts have been repeatedly worked over, and a sort of syncretism has everywhere invaded them. Men of the same name have been identified, peoples have been changed into individuals, many characters have dropped out of the story, the place and relationship of others have been altered, chronology has been confused, and there are besides gaps in the record. These points do not need illustration, but I may refer to the fact that Scandinavian tradition preserves no record of the Geatic kingdom, and consequentially none of those wars of Geats and Swedes which figure prominently in *Beowulf*.

At the time of Beowulf's encounter with the water-monsters the Danish throne is occupied by Hrothgar. He is represented as an old man ; if we take the words literally, a man of extreme old age. It is stated that he has held his kingdom secure against enemies for fifty years before Grendel's attacks began, also that these attacks had lasted for twelve years, that he had previously a successful reign of unstated duration, and that he succeeded his brother Heorogar. The latter was father of a son Heoroweard, apparently of an age to bear arms before his father's death, and he had possessed a certain sword ' for a long time ', but nevertheless Hrothgar obtained the throne in his youth. If all these statements are taken literally Hrothgar cannot have been far short of ninety ; at the lowest estimate he must have been over eighty years old. Gering in 1906 made a chronological table for the Geats based on state-ments in the poem taken literally, and on inferences from them,[1] but if we take into account the relations with other kings and peoples we are faced with irreconcilable diffi-culties for both Danes and Geats. It may be regarded as certain that the numbers are not to be accepted at their face value. Hrothgar received Beowulf's father at his court at the very beginning of his reign, say sixty-five years before the son visits him. Ecgtheow is dead, but if alive he must then have been about eighty-five. Beowulf is possibly not in his first youth, but he certainly is not a man of forty-five or fifty, and he must have been that or more if we adopt a literal interpretation. Furthermore, Hrothgar says explicitly that he was young. In the mouth of an old man young may not mean youthful, but it is absurd to suppose that he would apply the term to a man well advanced in middle age.

Rejecting such literal acceptance, there is nevertheless no doubt that the poet represents Hrothgar as far advanced in age. There are some slight discrepancies in the picture,

[1] In his German translation of *Beowulf*, pp. ix f.

but if we put aside inherent probabilities, not many. In one place a horse is prepared for him and he rides, in another we are told of a saddle which was his war-seat when he would engage in battle, and it is added that his skill in war never failed among the foremost when the corpses fell, and plainly it refers to the present. Finally, his wife, speaking of Hrothwulf and her sons, declares she is sure he will pay back to them in kindness the favour she and her husband showed him when a child if Hrothgar should die first, the other eventuality being apparently regarded as possible, and in fact, as far as we can judge, Hrothwulf must have been nearer in age to his uncle than to his cousins. These are indications of a different condition from that we get in the finished picture. Touching the question of inherent improbability, we note that Hrothgar has two sons who are in early youth. They sit among the young men and have no part, let alone a leading part, in state affairs, very unlike the prominence of their cousin. Wealhtheow speaks of them as of those unable effectively to assert their rights, and Beowulf's single allusion to the elder is appropriate to one who has not yet proved himself. There is also a daughter who is young and newly betrothed to Ingeld, whose youth also is fairly evident. These conditions are not impossible for a king who is already aged, but they are not likely without some special explanation. Rather they indicate a father in middle age but active and vigorous. This view is confirmed when other matters come into reckoning. As for Hrothwulf, if we give credence to the Scandinavian accounts, and without insisting too much on evidence so late, on this point they are likely to be based on sound tradition, then his father Halga must have been of extremely precocious development and his son midway between uncle and cousins. Hrothgar's sister was married to one of the Swedish dynasty, almost certainly Onela, and Onela was a contemporary of Beowulf's uncles Hæthcyn and Hygelac.

The sons of Onela's brother Ohthere were contemporaries more or less of Hygelac's son. If there is any truth in the story of Halga's incest, and it bears the mark of truth, then the sister can have been little younger than the brothers, but it is not easily credible that Onela would have had a wife so much older than himself as she must have been if Hrothgar were really old. Everything falls into place historically if we assume that in truth he was middle-aged, but it involves the conclusion that in Danish affairs at least we are not in an authentic historical atmosphere. On the contrary, the account is distorted in the interests of poetry, the imagination has been at work and transmuted the material. The discussion has been tedious, but the conclusion is weighty. We have to consider how far it is congruous with the history we find.

Pointed reference is made in *Beowulf* to the outbreak of strife between Hrothgar and his son-in-law. There are, moreover, continual allusions to the later action of Hrothwulf in seizing the throne, disregarding the claims of his cousins and without doubt killing them off. In the former case we should naturally gather from the poem that Heorot was attacked and fired by Ingeld and his Heathobeards. It is certain that it was attacked, but unsuccessfully. The evidence of *Widsith* puts the issue beyond doubt,[1] and it is unlikely that the hall succumbed in an unsuccessful attack. Moreover, the Scandinavian *Bjarkamál* makes it clear that the burning was connected with the internecine strife of the Scyldings after Hrothgar's death, and that is the sort of point on which the *Bjarkamál* can hardly be wrong. It will not do to think of a double destruction, the hall being re-erected in the interval ; the new hall would not be Heorot. The only admissible conclusion is that the poet was misinformed, and that means that he did not draw his information from sources trustworthy on his-

[1] Cf. K. Malone, *Widsith*, ll. 47–9.

torical detail. It is barely possible that in ll. 82 ff. we have two distinct events, the war with Ingeld and the burning, for the statements are too closely associated, and the order would be curious, but it is very possible that our poet has in error combined two distinct incidents in the life of the hall.

It is evident too that the situation at the Danish court is governed by the relation between uncle and nephew. It is not a likely or even a possible relation, even granting that Hrothwulf was a sister's son, that the pair should have occupied one hall in amity amid a retinue which owed allegiance to Hrothgar, or alternatively with two independent retinues (of which the poet knows nothing) occupying the hall side by side. We know from *Widsith* that they acted together at a time of national danger, and that there was close association is plain, but that does not imply the situation in the poem. It would have been for Hrothwulf a position of peculiar difficulty and danger, and for Hrothgar one of urgent disquiet, and examples early and late are too numerous for us to doubt how it would have been solved. If we look behind poetry to history we may safely infer that Hrothwulf had some special position and power in the Danish realm, and that he was too strong for Hrothgar to deal with him. The Hrothwulf of *Beowulf* is far removed from the *Hrolf* of Scandinavian tradition, who is more akin to Hrothgar and most likely has in fact taken over some of his uncle's characteristic traits. In *Beowulf* he is a silent and sinister figure in the background. We find beside him the evil counsellor Unferth, ' Unpeace, Strife ', a figment of poetry with a name no man would bear, and as Axel Olrik claimed on good grounds a figure invented for the Hrothwulf story.[1] He is the embodied attitude of Hrothwulf. Like other such evil advisers he is the personification of a sentiment, in this case Hrothwulf's jealous hatred. It is a recognized method of Germanic

[1] *The Heroic Legends of Denmark*, tr. L. M. Hollander, p. 58.

poetry. Instead of figuring internal conflict or evil passion in the individual, which would be difficult at that stage, it is given body and voice in the person of a zealous retainer. Even in the later English story of Ecgberht of Kent and his nephews we have Thunor as instigator and then perpetrator of the crime, though the details of the story leave no doubt of the responsibility. Unferth's claim to fame, the murder of kindred, is identical with the act which won Hrothwulf his kingdom, and we need have no doubt that Hrothwulf is characterized by his proxy.

Hrolf is exalted by Scandinavian tradition, but there are weighty grounds for doubting the position assigned him. His reign is empty of incident except the defence of Heorot and defeat of the Heathobeards (if Hothbroddus may be regarded as their equivalent), and his own defeat and death by Hiarvartus-Heoroweard. The other acts are a visit to Athils at Upsala, in which he appears in an undistinguished light in spite of the attempts of the sagas to get over it, and a slight connexion with Ali-Onela at the battle on Lake Wener. The essential part of the former is a folk-tale, and the probabilities are that he had nothing to do with either. In the latter point the sagas are at odds with *Beowulf*, and we should remember in regard to it that in the saga-period the Danish kingdom included a considerable part of what is now Sweden. Alfred's sailor Ohthere, coasting down from Christiania fjord, speaks of Denmark on his port, and says nothing of Sweden,[1] and this suggests that some of the land which once was Geatic was under Danish rule. There is then no difficulty in explaining the substitution of Danish for Geatic help to Athils-Eadgils at a time when the independent Geatic kingdom had long passed out of memory. It does not appear probable that Hrolf's reign was either long or glorious.

[1] King Alfred's *Orosius*, ed. H. Sweet (Early English Text Society, Orig. Series 79), p. 19.

What has happened is that his figure in which the dynasty of the Scyldings had, as it seemed to later days, its spectacular end, has absorbed the splendid traditions of the race, and stands out as at once its representative and culmination.

Hrothgar, too, is a figure of convention, determined by his place in the Hrothwulf story. I believe we can conclude that all the Danish material is at a long remove from history. Even in the wars of Dane and Heathobeards the favourite motives of poetry are forced into prominence, vengeance for kindred, futile marriage alliances, conflict of loyalties. It is clear from the report that they were already in the foreground, and Alcuin's passing reference to Ingeld confirms it. It is impossible to accept the poem as giving the true historical situation, and it is evident that Hrothgar has been touched by that tendency, so marked in the person of Charlemagne, to retreat in interest and activity compared with the members of his retinue, to become the hoary old king, in part with the wisdom, in part with the approaching senility of great age. Such a picture can only come from a developed heroic poetry, and our poet has inherited the traditional picture. It is not a direct and immediate transcript of reality, but transformed by successive handling, a reinterpretation of facts in the interest of emotional values.

The Geat material is more purely historical, less subject throughout to the intrusion of poetical motives. In the case of the Rhine-raid we saw how closely it adhered to history. The poet got his information from an historical lay, no doubt, but apart from the short interval between event and poem which helped to prevent distortion, more important is the simplicity of the content, incorporating none of those elements which, so to speak, corrupt the mass, none of those clashes which attract and then monopolize interest to the sacrifice of truth and proportion. The prowess of Beowulf may have become central so that he was glorified at the expense of others including the king, but even so historical accuracy is little impaired. The rest of the Geatic matter is of the same type and has the same chance of preserving accuracy in detail. There is one hint of other elements, but it is given incidentally and we have no clue to its bearing. It is a reference to Ongentheow's wife, the mother of his sons, who apparently was first rescued from the Geats, and then later perhaps lost again,[1] yet at that place the interest is concentrated on the details of a particular battle, not on the remoter causes which provoked or embittered the quarrel. The narrative of the later war, embracing Onela's attack on his nephew sheltering at the Geat court, and issuing in the death of one nephew Eanmund, and with him of the Geat king Heardred, followed by the reprisal of the surviving nephew Eadgils, aided by Beowulf now king, and the establishment of Eadgils on the Swedish throne, is all straightforward history, uninfluenced as far as can be seen by any extraneous poetical motives. In both cases accordingly the probabilities are great that the tradition has survived untainted. In the earlier phase Ongentheow's sons play an obscure part for which no explanation is forthcoming in the poem or elsewhere, and it is not impossible that in this great battle there is a telescoping of more than one encounter.

Scandinavian saga preserves no recollection of the Geat dynasty, no identification of names even which commands assent. Naturally it is otherwise with the Swedish, and incidents of Swedish history are remembered, but kings and history alike have suffered in the transmission, and the later accounts can be used only with caution to control or supplement *Beowulf*. Two things are evidently based on

[1] ll. 2930, 2954 ff.

old and sound tradition : in the poem, Hygelac's designation as *bona Ongenþeoes,* in the sagas, the name *Ottar
Vendilkråka* for Ohthere. Owing to gaps in the record
we cannot relate the two, but it is evident that the story
of Ottar's death at the hands of two brothers during an
attack on an enemy's kingdom has borrowed elements
from the fall of Ongentheow. In *Beowulf* we hear nothing
of the circumstances of Ohthere's death. Guessing from
what we are told, we should attribute it to his brother
Onela, but conjecture is idle in the absence of knowledge,
and possibilities are many. Though Ongentheow's name
has disappeared from the sagas, these confirm the poem
where they touch, and in the relations of Athils-Eadgils
and Ali-Onela the meagre allusion in *Beowulf* agrees with
the sagas except in the source of the assistance to Eadgils,
where it is certainly in the right, and it has preserved
accurate recollection of who Ali-Onela was, where the sagas
are entirely astray. It is the oldest record and where it
can be tested against other evidence the best informed,
and in short there need be no hesitation in accepting it
as accurate on matters of Geatic history.

That is an important result, in accord with an opinion
expressed years ago by Axel Olrik that the poet knew
Geat history, but only Danish heroic tradition as preserved
in poetry.[1] We have accounted for the historical accuracy
in the former by nearness to the events, in part also by
transmission in historical lays untouched or touched only
superficially by the popular motives of poetry. That is
not the whole story. It is impossible for the reader of
Beowulf to doubt that there is an acute and personal
interest in Geatic affairs. The impending outbreak between Hrothgar and his son-in-law is told impersonally and
dispassionately ; the attitude to Hrothwulf is a general
moral disapprobation ; but the narrative of Geat history

[1] *Op. cit.* p. 27.

71

past and to come is inspired by the active interest and undisguised feeling of one with his heart in the subject. At the same time it is useless to deny that there are difficulties in the account and unfortunately they are of a kind which cannot be controlled by independent evidence, since for the most part they affect the Geat dynasty alone. They have led, for example, to widely discrepant chronological schemes. The main point has to do with the age of Hrethel's sons and his grandson Beowulf, and consequentially the relative date of the battle of Ravenswood. At the time of the Heorot exploit Hygelac is said to be young and his wife Hygd very young. Beowulf himself refers to the king's youth in words which can be construed as almost patronizing. After the Ravenswood battle Hygelac had married his daughter to Eofor, while when killed on the Rhine-expedition he leaves a son so young that he cannot be safely entrusted with the kingdom, and Beowulf, refusing the throne, acts as guardian and regent. The youth of Hygelac and Hygd can conceivably be conventional, but the statements do not look in the least so, and the second marriage to which the chronologists have recourse may explain Hygd but not Hygelac. If Ravenswood preceded Beowulf's visit to Hrothgar, Hygd could not be both very young and the mother of a marriageable daughter some time previously. Hygelac could not be called young in those circumstances. At the same time the battle cannot be later, for Hæthcyn was killed there and succeeded by Hygelac, who was king at the time of Beowulf's exploit, and apparently had been so for some time. Beowulf's own reference to the battle proves that he had no part in it and suggests that it happened in his early youth. Some of his reputation for slackness, that is his tardy development, may be due to his absence. Hygelac was there and is to be regarded as rather older than Beowulf, yet more or less near to him in age, and Beowulf's remark on his youth is explicable on that assumption—

72

' though young (like myself) '. That Beowulf was young is certain from the manner of Hrothgar's allusion to him in ll. 1843 ff., and the natural inference from the following words is that Hygelac is older. Moreover, from his reception and treatment on his return it looks as if the affair of Grendel was his first exploit of significance, entitling him to the consideration he immediately receives. If these facts are so there is an error in the account, whatever the explanation may be, and Eofor's marriage with Hygelac's daughter is as much a fiction as the immensity of his reward.

Of greater moment and vital for theories regarding the genesis of the poem is the relation of Beowulf to the Geat dynasty. Hitherto I have spoken of him as if his existence and status could be taken for granted. It is true also that the conclusions previously advanced do not depend on either; they stand fast whoever he may have been or whencesoever he came into the story. In these days the view prevails that the relation of the hero to the Geats is a fiction of poetry, that Beowulf was not grandson of Hrethel, nephew of Hygelac, that no such person existed, and several recent discussions proceed on the assumption that his historical existence has been disproved. It is worth while considering anew the grounds on which the conclusion is based, and it is in regard to this question that in the foregoing I have emphasized the trustworthy character of Geat history in the poem. Deutschbein in an article gave expression, in the words of an English scholar, ' to the doubts which several had felt '[1] on the historicity of Beowulf. These doubts, and I include points not stressed by Deutschbein, are based on considerations like the following. Beowulf's name does not alliterate with his

---

[1] *Beowulf der Gautenkönig* in *Festschrift für L. Morsbach* (1913), pp. 291 ff. (Morsbachs Studien 50); and see R. W. Chambers, *Beowulf: An Introduction*, p. 531.

father's Ecgtheow, nor either with the Hrethlings, or as now more accurately stated with the Wægmundings. He is notably absent from the earlier phase of the Swedish war, having no part therein, and during a later phase, the attack on Heardred, he is again absent. In general, and this is the main point, the actions attributed to him are unreal and incredible, everything historical proceeds as if he did not exist, in fine, ' he is a prince of fairyland '. Too much stress can easily be laid on the practice of alliteration in names. The habit may well have been confined to reigning houses, and even there it is certainly not universal within the orbit of Scandinavian history. Ingeld of the Heathobeards does not alliterate with his father Froda, nor at a slightly earlier date Offa's name with his father Wermund. Further, I do not regard it as certain that Beowulf was a Wægmunding or that Wiglaf's relation to him was necessarily different from his own to Hygelac. The absence in the earlier phase of the Swedish war is at once clear if the chronology maintained in the previous part of this discussion is well founded. Beowulf was too young to intervene effectively. A special point is made by some of his absence during the attack on Heardred, and Deutschbein finds it especially incredible that he should have succeeded to the throne. Without going outside England there are parallels for both. What Deutschbein finds incredible happened in Northumbria when Oswald was killed, and in the other matter one might ask equally well where was Oswiu when his brother fell, and the Sussex nobles who subsequently made head against Ceadwalla. I also have some scepticism about the possibility of regency in the early sixth century, and the point may be the poet's, but it ought to be recognized that Beowulf was granted a semi-independent rule and his duties would lie elsewhere. In conquest in early times there were but two effective methods, settlement and incorporation, or else a tributary king. Oswiu tried a third method, govern-

ing Mercia through his own officers, but they were speedily
ejected, and that is what would have happened to any
alien Swedish dynasty of Wægmundings. Such objections
do not bear examination and the real case against Beowulf
is evidently based on the last point, the character of his
actions. When it is affirmed that everything proceeds as
if he were non-existent, I shall only say here that a definite
rôle is assigned to him in the Rhine-expedition and in
the matter of Eadgils. It is difficult to see what greater
precision or detail could be expected in a brief allusion.
The unreality, more properly the incredibility, of his
actions, the fairy-tale atmosphere which surrounds him is
the consequence of the folk-tale of which he is or has
become the hero, but it would be dangerous on that account
to conclude that he cannot have been a real person. Some
scholars who adopt this view favour also an identification
with Bothvar Bjarki. For that the only argument of
weight is the precision of the relation of each to Eadgils,
and provokes the criticism that the advocates wish to
have it both ways at once.

Consideration of some mediaeval romances may be fairly
recommended to those scholars who lay so much stress
on the miraculous character of Beowulf's acts. There is,
for example, a lengthy romance of Richard I, Richard of
the Lion Heart, belonging to the thirteenth century. The
history of Richard is as miraculous in its way as anything
in *Beowulf*. Starting with a strange story of his mother's
origin, it recounts how she flew away through the roof of
the church, in which she had been forcibly detained, on
the elevation of the host. She had by the hand John,
who fortunately fell and broke his thigh, and a daughter
who with the mother was never seen again. When Richard
appears events, even if they have contact with history,
pass into the realm of fantasy, become incredible and
even grotesque. He becomes king at fifteen on his father's

death from grief ; he was in reality thirty-two. During some extraordinary adventures in " Almain " just after his accession, he pushes his hand down the throat of a fierce lion sent to attack him, tears out heart and entrails, goes to the king's hall and squeezing out the blood salts and eats the heart, whence his name. Later he proceeds to Palestine, and there, while afflicted by a fever, he has a craving for pork where none can be had. Served in lieu with the flesh of a young and tender Saracen he eats greedily, and subsequently asks for the pig's head also. He is thereupon apprised of the deceit practised upon him, but only laughs and remarks that they should never die for lack of food. Help from St. George and angels, the latter especially in the management of a fiendish horse given him by Saladin for his destruction, capture of numerous cities like Babylon and Nineveh—all these and other things are given at length, but his reign after his return to England occupies four lines with two statements and one of them wrong. The inference should surely be that there was no Richard, that he is a figure foisted into the Plantagenet dynasty.

Argument from analogy is treacherous and an historical Richard does not prove an historical Beowulf, yet of the poems one confines itself professedly to human affairs, the other professedly does not. No doubt we have in *Beowulf* powers and performance beyond the capacity of humanity, and it is easy to lay stress on the incredible swimming feats, on the propensity of the hero to forgo weapons and crush his foe in an embrace. The latter at all events is not without parallel. Egil, son of Skallagrim, in circumstances not entirely dissimilar abandoned his useless weapons and clasping the enemy bit him through the neck.[1] On such things judgement is a matter of opinion and argument is idle, but I shall return to Beowulf's

[1] *Egils Saga Skallagrímsonar* c. 65.

supernatural feats. Meantime let us consider the question from another angle.

The subject is action remote from normal human activities. The stories are primaeval and world-wide. Obviously they were not invented for any man of the early sixth century, nor were originally associated with the historical setting in which we find them. Mythological interpretations used to be prevalent, but it has long been recognized and is now the accepted view that we have folk-tales heightened into literature. Everyone would agree to that, but then comes the parting of the ways. Two contending theories may be briefly examined. One, the older, makes Beowulf the substitute for and representative of an earlier figure, it makes no essential difference whether a divine heroic figure, or alternatively the nameless hero of the primitive folk-tale. Older scholars sought to connect the story of Grendel with Beow, whose name occurs in the genealogies as the son of Scyld, and they offered mythological interpretations of it, nature myths and culture myths. All of these are rightly rejected, but the Beow theory should not be identified with the mythological interpretation. It was suggested and supposed to be demonstrated by the collocation of the names Beowa (a weak form beside Beow) and Grendel in a Wiltshire Charter of 931.[1] There is a probability that the name Grendel was connected in England with a malicious and destructive water-monster, but the evidence falls short of proof, and it has been too readily assumed that Beowa of the charter and Beow of the genealogies are identical. That cannot possibly be proved. At the same time it should be noted that the name does not occur elsewhere, and, provided we may assume that weak and strong forms are variations of the same name, it would be a remarkable coincidence if they were different. If the weak

---

[1] W. de G. Birch, *Cart. Sax.* no. 677.

form is to be distinguished it must be a hypocoristic form, and names from which it could come are extremely uncommon. There is one Biuulf in the Durham *Liber Vitae* and a couple more can be traced in place-names, and that is all. In the introductory section of the poem Beowulf is substituted for Beow or Beowa by the author or by some scribe during transmission, and it seems to me more likely than not that the change was due to acquaintance with a story of Beow and Grendel which inspired the belief that Beowulf was the full form of the same name. These are guesses, yet the probabilities are after all in favour of an identification of Beow and Beowa. Nevertheless the identity is not necessary, nor is it even necessary to believe that Beow was associated with Grendel. The point in that claim is that it establishes a native English myth of very early date. For us the value lies in the easy transference of the story owing to association of names, and the attachment of floating stories to real persons is well authenticated in cases where no such special circumstance favours it. If there were an historical Beowulf the theory explains how such extraordinary stories came to be told of him. It offers no explanation of the genesis of the story ; that is a different question, of comparative mythology or folk-lore as the case may be.

The alternative theory proceeds differently and in the extreme form admits no substitution. Beowulf is the original hero of the folk-tale, and his name meaning ' bear ' indicates a half-animal strain in his nature. He is pushed into an historical situation with which he has nothing to do. There are difficulties in any theory, and it should be admitted that it is not possible to demonstrate the historicity of Beowulf, but the difficulties inherent in this theory seem to me inordinately great. A criticism of it may suggest grounds in favour of the alternative. The theory assumes of course that Beowulf is unhistorical and that this has been proved. The proof has been discussed. Leaving it aside, we have something like the introduction of our childhood stories into a precise historical setting, providing the heroes with place and connexions. We have as it were Tom Thumb or Jack the Giant-Killer made into the grandson of William the Conqueror, and made to play a part in sober history. One could believe only if analogous cases were cited. Romantic writers wished to make an English king of Havelok the Dane, but could find no credible place for him. It may be urged that these are not fair comparisons, that we are in the period of chronicles and records. Let us examine the case before us. The folk-tale hero Beowulf must have been transformed into a nephew of Hygelac at some period between the fall of the Geat kingdom and the composition of the epic. There are two possibilities. The identification was made by the poet or earlier. We must believe that *Beowulf* was meant for hearers or readers. It is not a literary exercise never intended to see the light. The history of the manuscript excludes a contrary view, and it is certain that it was known to some later poets. In that case it was designed for a society well acquainted with the heroic lays whence the poet got his knowledge. It is not readily credible that the poet could have introduced into a series of events known to the last detail an entirely alien figure, provided him with a carefully defined relationship to the ruling house, described in some detail his burial with all the pomp and circumstance proper to a king, referred to his burial-place in terms which suggest a familiar land-mark, familiar that is in the story, set him in direct associ-ation with another hero Breca, and his father in association with a real people, the Wylfings, both well known as subjects of other lays. To state the case is enough.

On the other hand, if Beowulf was already in the story, then he was a figure in the lays which underlie our epic.

At any point in their descent the introduction of the monster-slayer would be more difficult, the nearer the event the greater the difficulty. It must have been done within a century less or more of the fall of the kingdom or even of Hygelac's death. We have seen how accurately these events were remembered. Sons or grandsons of men who had lived through them heard of a grandson of Hrethel, a nephew of Hygelac, of whom not only historical tradition knew nothing, but also in the person of one familiar as the hero of a folk-tale. I say the men who lived through the events, for the original lays of the Geats, the struggles and the heroisms, must have originated amongst themselves, no matter when or how they passed to a wider circle. The history is too precise and too keenly felt to permit a different opinion. After the defeat, the destruction and absorption of the kingdom, the peasantry would remain under new rulers, but the surviving nobility must have gone into exile, in both cases just as at the overthrow of the Thuringian kingdom.[1] We are told so in the poem, a prophecy after the event, and evidently a record of fact. Lays of Geat heroes and Geat history, and especially lays of the struggle of Geat and Swede were composed and recited in the new home of the nobility wherever that may have been. Men who were noted sea-rovers, who made predatory expeditions as far as the Rhine, may well in part have come to England. I think it certain that the English element in Northumbria received some accession of strength about the middle of the sixth century, and perhaps from thence. Those who refuse the suggestion should find an explanation why Geat memories survived in England and there alone.

It may be said there is a weak link in the argument, the moment of the adoption of the lays into England, that

[1] *Sachsenspiegel* iii. 44 cited in Grimm, *Rechtsaltertümer* (2nd ed.), p. 322.

then and only then tradition might be set at defiance and an alien figure introduced. If the suggestion just offered is well founded there is no weak link. It cannot of course be proved that Geat exiles brought the lays with them. Putting that aside one must say that such violent alteration is not made at all events without some compelling motive, and certainly not at a time within memory of the events. Unexampled and inexplicable things occur, but we must deal with probabilities, and the chance of such alteration is remote. In general accordingly the intrusion of the hero of the folk-tale at the earlier date appears more incredible than at the later. Neither takes account of the fidelity with which genealogical details were treasured in memory in the heroic period. We may recall the words in *Hildebrandslied* : ' name me one of your kindred and I shall know the rest '.[1] Neither takes account of the accuracy of the history embedded in the poem, or of the jealous care with which the royal dynasties guarded the sanctity of kingship and kingly lineage. Beowulf is represented as king of the Geats with all the appurtenances of royalty, with a *comitatus* of whom one is named and set in relation to other men, including Beowulf himself. If he were such in the old lays he must have been so represented at a time when the reign was almost or quite within living memory. Chadwick has pointed out how at a much later period Scandinavians in Western Europe were meticulous in assuming the title of king.[2] It was confined to those of kingly descent and borne by men who in territory and power were not comparable with others who did not assume it because not royal. In an older period we have the attempt of Grimoald to displace the Merovingian Dagobert in favour of his son, unsuccessful though Dagobert was a mere puppet. We can cite still earlier the examples of Heruli and Cherusci. Even when not hereditary the king-

---

[1] l. 12. *ibu dû mî ẹnan sagês ik mî dê ôdre uuêt.*

[2] *Origin of the English Nation*, pp. 316-7.

ship was confined to a few kingly houses. The heroic society of seventh-century England, kings, princes and nobles in the midst of a living heroic tradition would not have tolerated such an intrusion. I do not see that we have any right to doubt that men then believed Beowulf to have been nephew of Hygelac and to have functioned as king of the Geats, and if that were the belief of heroic society in the seventh century, I do not see how it can have been anything but the truth. The imagination of the poet has without doubt been at work upon him, and round his name have gathered characteristic traits and actions which are not derived from history. His long and peaceful reign of fifty years can hardly be true to fact, while Hygelac's grant to him of a principality of seven thousand hides, and his relations with Heardred, look like the invention of the Anglo-Saxon poet. These are but embroidery on the authentic stuff of tradition.

I would not give an impression of certainty which I do not share. The validity of the argument depends on an hypothesis that *Beowulf* was written in the seventh century, and though previously I advanced considerations which lend it a high degree of probability, I do not venture to claim that they amount to proof. Notwithstanding the absence of stringent proof, I do claim that the former theory of a real person attracting floating stories agrees better with the facts and ought to be accepted. One result issues from the attachment. In respect of the folk-tale element the real person is transported into the realm of fantasy, most of all when the historical is deliberately made subordinate. In *Beowulf* the folk-tale *is* the story : all the rest is incidental. That has its effect on the manner in which every activity of the hero is imagined. Some of Beowulf's actions are accentuated in the direction of the unreal, the supernatural, in particular since in im-mediate contact with historical circumstance, his swimming home with thirty suits of armour. It may be we take the words too literally and that the Anglo-Saxon understood well enough what was meant, as we understand the phrase that So-and-so carried off the prize when there is no carrying nor any tangible prize. It is fairly clear that Beowulf did have to swim. Apart from all that there is no doubt that the historical figure has been touched by elements which issue from no historical source, and it is idle to claim that their influence is present only when the circumstance is itself of a different world from history. He is of necessity projected into a world of figments, an unreal territory governed by the imagination and subject to other laws than those of ordinary life, and so subject however active the belief, constant and profound the conviction in the existence of demons, spirits of evil, monsters and dragons, or all the host of maleficent shapes of horror and darkness. As their powers transcend mortal capacity so must his resource be enlarged and transmuted into something more than human, even as the effluence of the divine lingered round the early saints and martyrs, and endowed them with senses and powers beyond those natural to man. It is on such lines that Beowulf must be judged. Shall we discredit the early saints of the Church or reject their historical activities because we refuse belief to the extraordinary, even grotesque acts or behaviour not seldom attributed to them ? They too were eminently occupied with things beyond the boundary of sense, or at all events outside the range of normal experience, with inevitable reaction on the manner of their portrayal. If all Beowulf's actions were marked by this aloofness from the restraints of human nature we might be compelled to a different conclusion. It is not so. Confessedly, there is matter for wonder and scope for doubt, but we might be able to answer with complete satisfaction some of the questionings which rise in men's minds over the poet's presentment of his hero if we could also answer with certainty the question why he chose just this subject, when to our modern judgment there were at hand so many greater, charged with the splendour and tragedy of humanity, and in all respects worthier of a genius as astonishing as it was rare in Anglo-Saxon England.

IV

SUTTON HOO AND THE
BACKGROUND TO THE POEM

by Rupert Bruce-Mitford

ARCHAEOLOGY is the sole branch of Dark Age studies (to use a convenient term) in which the documents are being continually augmented—by the discovery of new antiquities and structures. This is true especially of the pagan centuries of the Germanic peoples, when things were placed in the grave to accompany the dead—centuries for which other kinds of documents scarcely exist. The standards of Germanic archaeology have also in recent years become more critical. Technological advances in the Research Laboratory and the conservation workshop have provided new means of appraising old finds and new. Since 1935, when *Beowulf and the Seventh Century* was published, the archaeological picture of the relevant centuries has in consequence become a good deal clearer. So far as *Beowulf* is concerned this new clarity is being created, above all, by the Sutton Hoo ship-burial discovered near Woodbridge, in Suffolk, in 1939—only four years after Professor Girvan's book appeared.

It is the purpose of this chapter to show how Girvan's discussion of the background of the poem (Chapter II) is affected by the Sutton Hoo discovery. The chapter does not set out to give a balanced treatment of *Beowulf and Archaeology*, nor to take up a position upon the difficult,

perhaps insoluble, questions of the poem's date and provenance, although it naturally stresses the possible significance of Sutton Hoo in these connections.

In considering the relevance of Sutton Hoo to *Beowulf*
we need, in the first place, to be clear as to the date at
which the burial took place. The purse in the burial-deposit
held thirty-seven Merovingian gold coins. These always
seemed to offer the best hope of dating the burial, but it is
only recently that fundamental advances in the field of
Merovingian numismatics have enabled us to reach a firm
conclusion. The coins, it can now be said, were almost
certainly assembled no later than c. A.D. 620–625.[1] The
coins, it is true, only provide a *terminus post quem* ; the
assemblage might have been kept intact for any length of
time before it came to be buried. But the burial can hardly
be much later, on historical grounds. Because of the
establishment of Christianity in the East Anglian royal
house a king's burial (as this seems to be) in a pagan grave-
field is very unlikely after c. A.D. 635. The ship-burial may,
after all, as was originally suggested, be that of the greatest
of the East Anglian kings, Redwald, who seems to have died
in A.D. 625 or 626.[2]

The date favoured by Girvan for the making of *Beowulf*
was not earlier than 670, and most probably A.D. 680–700
(p. 25). If this were correct, it could mean that the poem
had been composed within living memory of the Sutton
Hoo ship-burial.[3]

[1] A detailed exposition of the new dating is given in Volume I
of the British Museum definitive publication (forthcoming) on the
Sutton Hoo discovery.

[2] H. M. Chadwick, ' Who was he ? ' *Antiquity*, XIV, 1940, Section
VIII.

[3] An eighth-century date for Beowulf is now generally advocated
and is best argued in Dorothy Whitelock's *The Audience of Beowulf*.

Girvan's dating is based essentially on the conviction that the only suitable place of origin for so sophisticated and civilized a poem was Northumbria of the ' golden age '.

In his review of the archaeology of the poem Girvan is especially concerned to counter the view that it reflects the customs and manners of the Migration period (c. A.D. 350–550). In *Beowulf*, practices and objects are described which Girvan supposed to belong to this early age—or at least to be contemporary with the historical events alluded to in the poem, i.e. of the early sixth century. He argued that these early elements were not evidence for a date of composition earlier than that which he favoured because they were covered at best in vague language, lacking the familiar touch of personal knowledge. ' I shall endeavour to show that little or no trustworthy evidence of life and manners in the Migration period, as distinct from later times, can be derived from the poem ' (p. 32).

The Sutton Hoo burial supports Girvan's attempt to detach *Beowulf* from the later Migration period (though not his arguments for doing so) by demonstrating that what he took to be archaic elements in a late seventh-century poem were not archaic ; they are consistent with the century to which he would like to attribute the poem, the seventh.

Corrections to Girvan in this respect may be quickly made. Thus of Scyld's funeral he wrote (p. 33) :

It is impossible that the poet had personal knowledge or direct information . . . it ought not to be forgotten that ship-burial was obsolete long before the sixth century. The ancient founder of the house of the Scyldings was buried in an obsolete way.

It is true that Scyld's funeral-ship was not buried but abandoned to the sea, a practice which, if it ever existed in fact, has naturally left no trace. In the poem it may be seen as a mythical or literary element, Scyld's departure made as mysterious as his arrival. At all events the distinction between being buried and set adrift is not made by Girvan, who speaks of Scyld's funeral simply as a ship-burial. It represents, in effect, the ship-burial idea, the dead man being placed in his vessel for his last journey, and richly provided with belongings and symbols of his status.

The Sutton Hoo burial shows at any rate that ship-inhumation, with provision of grave-goods similar to that of Scyld, was being practised in an Anglo-Saxon setting, in a royal context and on a scale comparable with Scyld's funeral, as late as the second quarter of the seventh century; that is to say, within reach of the period to which Girvan would attribute the composition of the poem.

Again, Girvan refers to ' the damascened swords, no longer made '. We now know from the application of radiography to oxidised iron that these resilient pattern-welded blades continued to be made regularly down to the tenth century. The two swords so far represented at Sutton Hoo both had blades of this type.[1]

In the Sutton Hoo burial was also one of the rarest of Anglo-Saxon grave-goods, a corselet, or coat of mail; it survives only as a folded mass of rusted links. There is no justification for Girvan's comment ' the corselet of chain in Beowulf must have been a survival '. He was influenced in saying this by the many corselets supposedly of provincial Roman origin, now in the Schloss Gottorp Museum, Schleswig, from the Nydam and Thorsberg bog-finds, showing this type of body-armour to be typical of the fourth century; but evidently such corselets, with

[1] The tip of a sword-blade was found in the boat-grave excavated in 1938. (*Proceedings of the Suffolk Institute of Archaeology*, XXX, 1964, Pl. VIII ; p. 26, No. 8.)

the same alternating rows of welded and riveted links, continued in use in aristocratic Germanic circles. The Sutton Hoo example is matched by chain-mail in Swedish seventh- and eighth-century boat-graves, including mail curtains attached to the caps of helmets as neck-protectors, and explaining, as Rosemary Cramp has established, the phrase *befongen fraewrasnum* (circled with noble chains) as applied to a helmet.[1]

There is no reason to suppose that the use of corselets like that at Sutton Hoo did not continue to the Norman Conquest. Here, as with much else, the Sutton Hoo find demonstrates that the poet's knowledge need be sought no further afield and no earlier than seventh-century England.

Another point that struck Girvan was that in the account of the burials of both Scyld and Beowulf, nothing is said ' of horse, hawk or hound[2] or wife or slaves, male or female ' (p. 33).

Such Scandinavian ship-burials as that of the Russ (or Swedish Viking) chieftain cremated on the Volga (pp. 36–38) or the Queen's ship-inhumation at Oseberg, in Norway, or that of an early Norse settler in the Isle of Man,[3] show that slaves were sacrificed to accompany the dead ; and in the Viking ship-burial at Ladby in Denmark, and the earlier Vendel-age boat-graves in Sweden—at Vendel itself

[1] Rosemary Cramp, Beowulf and Archaeology, in *Medieval Archaeology*, Volume I, 1957, pp. 57–77, and reprinted in Donald K. Fry, *The Beowulf Poet*, 1968, pp. 114–40.

[2] Dorothy Whitelock has noted the fondness of the Anglo-Saxon upper classes for hunting and fowling, and alluded to the references in *Beowulf* to stag and boar hunting and hawking (*The Audience of Beowulf*, 1964, pp. 92–3).

[3] Gerhard Bersu and D. M. Wilson, *Viking burials in the Isle of Man*, Society for Medieval Archaeology Monographs, No. I, pp. 55–61.

and at the more scientifically investigated Valsgärde—a wide range of animals including bulls, saddle horses, leashes of dogs, falcons, an eagle owl and a tame crane have been identified.[1] This solemn and colourful sacrifice of living things in the provision for the dead was regular Scandinavian practice from early times, both with inhumation and cremation burials.

It is thus indeed a peculiarity in the poem, as Girvan saw, that there is no reference to any such practices in its accounts of what purport to be important Scandinavian burials. Girvan suggested that this, along with other omissions, was part of a ' policy of deliberate suppression by the poet of all that is shocking to Christian sentiment ' (p. 33). It is perhaps more likely to be a reflection of the funeral rites of late pagan times in the milieu in which the poem took shape, for absence of human and animal sacrifice was characteristic of rich Anglo-Saxon and Continental Germanic inhumations in the sixth and seventh centuries. What is of interest is that at Sutton Hoo we find this absence in the Anglo-Saxon milieu, in a royal ship-burial of an east-Scandinavian type containing Swedish elements.[2]

[1] H. Stolpe and T. J. Arne, *La Necropole de Vendel*, Stockholm, 1927, pp. 8–9.

[2] Shield, helmet, sword (but not scabbard) and loose ' sword-ring ' are all of Swedish make.

At Sutton Hoo the soil conditions were such that inhumed bone might have disappeared without trace. Nevertheless, the absence of any metal elements from animal harness, or fittings or equipment that might have been associated with a second person, and negative chemical evidence derived from the grave-goods, justify a firm conclusion that no remains of inhumed animals were present—certainly not on a scale commensurate with the rest of the grave furniture. A possibility that the Sutton Hoo burial was a cenotaph, and therefore abnormal, remains. But this would hardly of itself explain the absence of sacrificial animals or humans, when it was nevertheless thought fit to sacrifice so much treasure.

Again, Girvan thought that the failure in the poem to mention the firing of Scyld's vessel showed lack of direct knowledge. In literary accounts from later saga sources, collected by Stjerna, of funeral ships abandoned to the sea, the ships were fired.[1]

As has been said, there is no archaeological record of this practice. Stjerna pointed out long ago[2] that there are plenty of examples of unburnt ship-burials of the pre-Viking age in Scandinavia. The Sutton Hoo burial (with the only two other known examples of pre-Viking ship-burial from the British Isles, both from the same corner of Suffolk, that recognized at Sutton Hoo in 1938 and another found at Snape in 1862[3]) shows that unburnt ship-burials were known to the Anglo-Saxons in the early seventh century.

These features, discussed by Girvan, may be taken then as reflecting Anglo-Saxon society of the early seventh century, rather than as implying ignorance, remoteness or any distaste for pagan practices on the part of the poet or his audience. The poem is reinforced as to its plausibility, consistency, artistic integrity and setting.

* * *

Archaeologists must not claim too much for their discoveries, lest they mislead colleagues in other fields of study, or worse, cause the evidence itself to be underestimated. Equally, literary and linguistic scholars must be careful not to get carried away by enthusiasm in finding

[1] K. Stjerna, *Essays on Beowulf*, trs. J. R. Clark Hall, 1912, p. 112.
[2] *Op. cit.* pp. 126–7 (Stjerna's chronological sequence of types of funeral practice associated with ships, however, is invalid).
[3] R. L. S. Bruce-Mitford, The Snape Boat-Grave, *Proceedings of the Suffolk Institute of Archaeology*, XXVI (1952).

in archaeological evidence interpretations of detail in the
poem, when archaeologists themselves are aware of the
deficiencies of that evidence. An example, not meant with
disrespect, may be taken from a distinguished contributor
to *Beowulf* studies, the late Professor C. L. Wrenn, who
wrote :

Indeed the royal standard, though of course the gold embroidery
of the Sutton Hoo exemplar has left no trace, with all its complicated
ritual symbolising victory, protection, death, etc. as it waved over
the King's treasure in death as in life, is a marked feature alike in
Sutton Hoo and in Beowulf. Both in the cenotaph and in the poem
it always implies royalty and treasure,

and :

If we may judge of the exquisite delicacy and beauty of the gold and
inlaid purse frame of the Sutton Hoo cenotaph, the purse itself
must have been made of wondrously embroidered cloth of gold,
as must also the standard, whose iron frame alone survives.[1]

It is perhaps unfair in me to point out how many questions this passage begs. Is the object certainly a standard ?
If so, does not Bede suggest the knowledge of three different
types (*signum*, *vexillum*, *tufa*), two evidently used by
Anglo-Saxon Royalty ?[2] This top-heavy iron affair with
volutes to either side of its point for driving it into the
ground is not the kind of thing that one would expect to
find attached to the mast, *heah ofer heafod*.[3] Again, is

[1] *Mélanges de Linguistique et de Philologie ; Fernand Mossé in
memoriam*, ' Sutton Hoo and Beowulf ', pp. 489–9 : reprinted in
Lewis E. Nicholson, *An Anthology of Beowulf Criticism*, University
of Notre Dame Press, 1963, pp. 311–30.

[2] Bk. II, Chapter 16.

[3] p. 34: There remains the question of the mast, which comes
in twice, supporting the body, and carrying the golden standard
' high over his head '; cf. Stjerna, *op. cit.*, p. 130, on the *segn* in
Scyld's funeral ship : ' It was fastened to a long pole . . . probably
made fast to the mast also ' (Klaeber, Third Edition, with supplement, 1941, p. 127, note 47).

the object, or the grave, certainly royal ?[1] Is the monument really a cenotaph ?

Without answering these questions there is one thing that we can be sure about in connection with the Sutton Hoo iron stand. Whatever the explanation of its unique design may be, there never was any gold embroidery associated with it, nor was there with the purse. The gold threads of Anglo-Saxon embroideries invariably survive in all soil conditions, and in a properly conducted excavation are invariably found.[2] Indeed the rusted iron stand is conspicuously free from textile impressions of any sort. No gold embroidery hung above the Sutton Hoo hoard.

Again, Wrenn wrote ' the standard of the dragon, like that of Sutton Hoo, was already ancient when buried '. It is possible, as I have suggested elsewhere,[3] that the bronze stag associated with the iron stand at Sutton Hoo may be an exotic antique, but there is no evidence that the object itself, the putting of the stag (a treasured antique) on top of this iron pedestal, creating a ' standard ', is old. Indeed it now appears doubtful whether the bronze stag was ever mounted on the iron stand at all.[4]

Yet, when the same author claims for the Sutton Hoo discovery that ' it may well seem the most important

[1] J. M. Wallace-Hadrill, The Graves of Kings, *Studi Medievali* 3 Ser. I, 1, Spoleto, 1960 (Centro Italiano di Studi sull' alto medioevo).

[2] Elisabeth Crowfoot and Sonia Chadwick Hawkes, Early Anglo-Saxon Gold Braids, *Medieval Archaeology*, XI, 1967, pp. 42–86. Quantities of gold thread from braids can be seen with the Taplow Barrow finds in the British Museum.

[3] *Proceedings of the Suffolk Institute of Archaeology*, XXV, 1949, p. 11.

[4] This point is dealt with fully in the forthcoming Volume I of the British Museum definitive publication of the ship-burial.

happening' (in *Beowulf* studies) 'since the Icelander Jón
Grímur Thorkelin made his transcripts of the *Beowulf* MS
and from then published the first edition of the poem '[1],
it would not be surprising if time did not show him to
be right. This we will return to shortly.

The correspondence between the provisions for the dead
at Sutton Hoo and that for Scyld described in the poem—
the ship itself, the weapons and armour (spears, sword,
mailcoat, helmet, shield and dagger), the gold, the symbols
of tribal power or office (ðeodgestreon, ðeodenmathmas)
the treasures from far—need not of itself be of special
significance. Similar provision occurs in Scandinavian
boat-graves of the seventh and eighth centuries A.D. and
no doubt occurred in the royal burials of the time. Even
the specific nature of certain correspondences, for example
between helmets described in the poem and the Sutton
Hoo helmet, need not mean anything special. Isolated
parallels can always occur, and are found in other Germanic
graves. The only surviving helmet with a boar-crest, for
example (though itself not of the Swedish helmet-type
described in *Beowulf* and found at Sutton Hoo), occurs
in the Benty Grange tumulus, in Derbyshire ; one of two
known sword-pommels with runic inscription in a grave
at Gilton, in Kent, to choose Anglo-Saxon examples.[2]
What seems significant is the hitherto unlooked-for con-
centration of such parallels, including reflections of Christianity[3] and lack of funeral sacrifice, in a royal ship-burial
of Scandinavian type in a civilized Anglo-Saxon setting.

[1] C. L. Wrenn, in his supplement ' Sutton Hoo and Beowulf '
to the Third Edition of R. W. Chambers, *Beowulf—An Introduction
to the Study of the Poem*, 1967, p. 508, *et seq.*

[2] See H. E. Davidson in Garmonsway and Simpson, *Beowulf and
Its Analogues*, pp. 354–6.

[3] The spoons, silver bowls with cruciform designs, crosses in the
scabbard bosses etc.

Two of the Sutton Hoo finds, however, may be singled out here as having a special interest.

Since Professor J. C. Pope published in 1942 his theory of the use of the harp to fill initial rests and provide a regular beat in Old English Poetry—to organize its rhythm —interest has attached to the kind of instrument this was, and to the sort of accompaniment it might have provided. When Pope wrote, he felt it necessary to say ' we may never know, and perhaps can never even conjecture, just what the musical accompaniment was like '. He speculated a little on how ' the small harp then in use ' may have been used. Now the Sutton Hoo burial contained the remains of a six-stringed instrument of music which has recently been, it seems, validly reconstructed.[1] We seem justified in claiming it as the instrument called in *Beowulf hearpe*, although it is not technically a harp, but a round lyre. The recovery from the Sutton Hoo burial of the instrument used to accompany the performance, and even to assist or condition the composition, of early Anglo-Saxon poetry, even if we do not know how it was tuned, and no note of music survives from this era, should enable practical experiments to be carried out on a valid basis. It becomes possible to demonstrate the capacities of the instrument, and allow of sounder thoughts on its possible relevance to the problems of Old English prosody, and its role in Anglo-Saxon courtly life.

Secondly, the Sutton Hoo helmet provides the closest analogy yet with those described in *Beowulf*. It is the self-same type, and of Swedish make. It is the only Germanic masket helmet. It was shining and silver-coloured (*hwit*), its surface being tinned. Boar-images are set over the cheek-pieces ; and it provided an unexception-

---

[1] *Antiquity*, XLIV, 1970, pp. 7–13.

able explanation of the word *walu*,[1] as referring to the thick external iron crest which runs over the top of the helmet from front to back. Even if the Sutton Hoo helmet may be old—an heirloom, perhaps an historic battle-trophy–its presence in the Sutton Hoo burial shows that the type was known to courtly circles in East Anglia in the seventh century.[2]

* * *

The potential of the Sutton Hoo discoveries for Beowulf studies, however, may be found to rest not so much on such analogies in themselves as on the clue that the ship-burial as a whole may provide to the poem's place of composition and to the transmission of its Scandinavian themes to the Anglo-Saxon milieu—two of the major problems to do with the poem still unsolved. The excavation of the remaining burial-mounds at Sutton Hoo may well yield discoveries that will strengthen the case for a possible East Anglian origin of the poem, a possible origin which must now be given serious consideration.

Sutton Hoo has revealed a level of sophistication and material culture at the East Anglian court not suspected hitherto ; it was a milieu capable of producing the finest gold jewellery of its era to survive in Europe, having wide contacts (treasures from afar—Frankish coins, Byzantine silver, Coptic and Celtic bowls, etc.), and Scandinavian links so strong, it seems, as to indicate very plausibly for the Wuffingas (the East Anglian royal house) dynastic origins in Sweden.[3]

[1] R. Bruce-Mitford in R. H. Hodgkin, *A History of the Anglo-Saxons*, 3rd Edition, Volume II, pp. 762–4; Beowulf, 1030–4.

[2] For a detailed discussion of helmet see Rosemary Cramp, ' Beowulf and Archaeology ' in *Medieval Archæology*, I, 1957, reprinted in Donald K. Fry, *The Beowulf Poet*, Prentice-Hall Inc. 1968 (see pp. 119–25).

[3] Cf. R. H. Hodgkin, *A History of the Anglo-Saxons*, 3rd Edition,

It seems therefore that an archaeological context has appeared with a particular relevance not matched elsewhere. With this should be taken into account certain evidence from place-names and the royal genealogy.[1]

We have no knowledge of East Anglian culture at this later time, to set beside what we know of the achievement of Northumbria or Mercia, but the Christian monastic foundations continued to prosper,[2] and the Wuffinga dynasty survived through a period of irreversible political decline.

There is scope in East Anglian history for pride in lineage and for a nostalgic looking-back in decline to days of greatness, qualities of *Beowulf* which Girvan thought particularly appropriate to the Northumbria of the end of the seventh century.

Schücking's attempt to date *Beowulf* to the end of the ninth century[3] and to find a setting for the poem in the

---

1952, pp. 719–24, Wrenn, *loc. cit.* pp. 512–13. J. L. N. O'Loughlin, Sutton Hoo—the evidence of the documents, *Medieval Archaeology*, Vol. 8, 1964, pp. 1–19. R. L. S. Bruce-Mitford, *The Sutton Hoo Ship-Burial—a Handbook*, British Museum, 1968, pp. 69–71, Lindqvist, Sutton Hoo and Beowulf, *Antiquity*, XX, 1948, pp. 131–40.

[1] G. Sarrazin as long ago as 1899 suggested that Norfolk and Suffolk were settled by a branch of the northern tribe known as Wylfings (O'Loughlin, *op. cit.*, p. 5, Lindqvist, *op. cit.*).

[2] As at Ely, St. Botulph's monastery at Icanhoh (Iken, near Snape, is a very probable location), founded by Aethelhere and Aethelwald, according to one source, in 654, obtained a reputation for organization and efficiency such that it was specially visited by Coelfrith (the future Abbot of Monkwearmouth and Jarrow) shortly after A.D. 669 (F. M. Stenton, *Anglo-Saxon England*, p. 117), before the Jarrow-Wearmouth venture was launched.

[3] Wann entstand der Beowulf ? Glossen, Zweifel und Fragen, *Beiträger zur Geschichte der Deutschen Sprache*, X/ii, 1917, 347–410. Apparently, still taken seriously by some authorities, although I can see nothing at all to recommend it.

Court of an Anglo-Danish king in the Danelaw, was stimu-
lated by the need to find a substantial motive for 'the
very remarkable interest taken in matters Scandinavian '.[1]

' This,' Klaeber said, ' still calls for an adequate explanation. It is something that has ever haunted scholars since
the days of Thorkelin and Thorpe.' Earlier, Klaeber wrote
of the ubiquitous Scandinavian elements in the Old English
poem, ' it is not their mere presence that has to be accounted
for but their curiously historical character '. He quoted
Morsbach's speculation :

The most satisfying explanation offered by way of a hypothesis
is that there may have existed close relations perhaps through
marriage between an Anglian court and the Kingdom of Denmark,
whereby a special interest in Scandinavian traditions was fostered
among the English nobility.

If the East Anglian royal house, the Wuffingas, were of
direct Swedish or Geatish origin, would this not supply the
required motive ? And is this not reinforced by the nature
of the evidence which enables us to suggest it, viz. the
discovery in Suffolk of a royal ship-burial—very likely that
of the greatest of the dynasty—containing objects of
Swedish origin virtually identical (where we can check)
with objects described in the poem ?

When we have a single long poem that deals with royal
and secular society in the pre-Viking age and a single royal
grave (as we suppose) of the pre-Viking period, we must
be careful not to force the obvious relevance of the one to
the other into a dual reflection of the same milieu. But
it may well seem that at Sutton Hoo we have something
more than this. It is the unique nature of the Swedish
connection revealed by the Sutton Hoo burial that seems
to open up the possibility of a direct link.

[1] F. Klaeber, *Beowulf and the Fight at Finnsburg* (1941 edition),
Introduction, pp. cxxiii, cxv, etc.

SELECT BIBLIOGRAPHY

1 Bibliographies

Comprehensive bibliographies are provided in Klaeber's edition of the poem (see 3 below) up to 1948, in Chambers' *Introduction* (see 5 below) up to 1958, and by D. K. Fry, *Beowulf and The Fight at Finnsburh: A Bibliography* (Charlottesville, 1969) up to 1967. These may be supplemented by *The Annual Bibliography of English Language and Literature* published for the Modern Humanities Research Association, *The Year's Work in English Studies* published for the English Association, *P.M.L.A. Annual Bibliography* published for the Modern Language Association, *Abstracts of English Studies* published for the National Council of Teachers of English, and The Year's Work in Old English Studies published in the *Old English Newsletter*.

2 Manuscript and Transcripts

The manuscript, British Museum Cotton Vitellius A. XV fols. 129 (132)a to 198 (201)b, has twice been published in facsimile:

J. Zupitza, *Beowulf: Autotypes of the Unique Cotton MS. Vitellius, A. XV in the British Museum, with a Transliteration*, Early English Text Society, Old Series 77 (London, 1882); 2nd ed., with introduction by N. Davis, E.E.T.S. 245 (London, 1958).

K. Malone, *The Nowell Codex*, Early English Manuscripts in Facsimile XII (Copenhagen, 1963).

The manuscript was scorched by fire in 1731, and valuable information can be derived from two transcripts made in 1787 before the damage to the edges of the pages became as extensive as it is now:

K. Malone, *The Thorkelin Transcripts of Beowulf*, Early English Manuscripts in Facsimile I (Copenhagen, 1951). The following studies are also important:

M. Förster, ' Die Beowulf-Handschrift ' *Berichte über die Verhandlungen der Sächsischen Akademie der Wissenschaften zu Leipzig, LXXI*, 4 (1919).

K. Sisam, *Studies in the History of Old English Literature* pp. 61–96, 289–90 (Oxford, 1953).

3 Editions

The four most important and informative modern editions are:

F. Klaeber, *Beowulf and The Fight at Finnsburg*, 3rd ed. with First and Second Supplements (Boston, 1951).

E. van K. Dobbie, *Beowulf and Judith*, The Anglo-Saxon Poetic Records IV (New York and London, 1953).

C. L. Wrenn, *Beowulf and the Finnesburg Fragment*, 2nd ed. (London and Boston, 1958).

E. von Schaubert, *Heyne-Schückings Beowulf neubearbeitet*, 18th ed. (Paderborn, 1961–3).

4 Translations

Beowulf has often been translated: there are renderings by, amongst others, Longfellow (selections) and William Morris. Special mention may be made of the following modern versions:

J. Clark Hall and C. L. Wrenn, *Beowulf and the Finnsburg Fragment : A translation into Modern English Prose*, new revised ed. (London, 1950).

E. Morgan, *Beowulf: A Verse Translation into Modern English* (New York, 1953).

SELECT BIBLIOGRAPHY

D. Wright, *Beowulf: A Prose Translation with an Intro-duction* (London and Baltimore, 1957).

K. Crossley-Holland, *Beowulf*, with an introduction by B. Mitchell (London, 1968).

G. K. Garmonsway and J. Simpson, *Beowulf and its Analogues*, including ' Archaeology and *Beowulf* ' by H. E. Davidson (London and New York, 1968).

5 Interpretation and Criticism

In addition to the introductions to the editions and trans-lations listed above, the following works will be found especially helpful:

W. P. Ker, *Epic and Romance*, 2nd ed. (New York and London, 1908).

H. M. Chadwick, *The Heroic Age* (Cambridge, 1912).

W. W. Lawrence, *Beowulf and Epic Tradition* (Cam-bridge, Mass., 1928).

J. Hoops, *Beowulfstudien* (Heidelberg, 1932).

J. Hoops, *Kommentar zum Beowulf* (Heidelberg, 1932).

J. R. R. Tolkien, ' Beowulf : the Monsters and the Critics ' *Publications of the British Academy*, XXII, pp. 245–95 (1936) ; also separately printed (London, 1937), and included in Nicholson's *Anthology* and Fry's *Collection* (see below).

A. Bonjour, *The Digressions in Beowulf*, Medium Aevum Monographs V (Oxford, 1950).

D. Whitelock, *The Audience of Beowulf* (Oxford, 1951).

R. W. Chambers, *Beowulf: An Introduction to the Study of the Poem, with a Discussion of the Stories of Offa and Finn*, 3rd ed. with a Supplement by C. L. Wrenn (Cam-bridge, 1959).

A. G. Brodeur, *The Art of Beowulf* (Berkeley and Los Angeles, London, 1959).

G. V. Smithers, *The Making of Beowulf* (Durham, 1961).

A. Bonjour, *Twelve Beowulf Papers 1940–1960, with Additional Comments* (Neuchatel, 1962).

L. E. Nicholson (ed.), *An Anthology of Beowulf Criticism* (Notre Dame, 1963).

S. B. Greenfield (ed.), *Studies in Old English Literature in Honor of A. G. Brodeur* (Eugene, Oregon, 1963).

K. Sisam, *The Structure of Beowulf* (Oxford, 1965).

J. A. Leake, *The Geats of Beowulf* (Madison, 1966).

E. G. Stanley, ' Beowulf ' *Continuations and Beginnings*, pp. 104–41, ed. E. G. Stanley (London, 1966).

D. K. Fry (ed.), *The Beowulf Poet: A Collection of Critical Essays* (New Jersey, 1968).

E. B. Irving, *A Reading of Beowulf* (New Haven and London, 1968).

M. E. Goldsmith, *The Mode and Meaning of Beowulf* (London, 1970).

6 Language, Style and Metre

In addition to the introductions to the editions listed above, the following works may be noted:

E. Sievers, *Altgermanische Metrik* (Halle, 1893).

C. W. M. Grein and J. J. Köhler, *Sprachschatz der angelsächsischen Dichter* (Heidelberg, 1912).

H. C. Wyld, ' Diction and Imagery in Anglo-Saxon Poetry ', *Essays and Studies*, XI, pp. 49–91 (1925).

S. O. Andrew, *Postscript on Beowulf* (Cambridge, 1948).

K. Sisam, *Studies*, pp. 119–39 (see 2 above).

F. P. Magoun, ' The Oral-formulaic Character of Anglo-Saxon Narrative Poetry ', *Speculum*, XXVIII, pp. 446–67 (1953); also included in Nicholson's *Anthology* and Fry's *Collection* (see 5 above).

A. J. Bliss, *The Metre of Beowulf* (Oxford, 1958).

A. Campbell, ' The Old English Epic Style ', *English and Medieval Studies Presented to J. R. R. Tolkien on the Occasion of his Seventieth Birthday*, pp. 13–26, edd. N. Davis and C. L. Wrenn (London, 1962).

R. Quirk, ' Poetic Language and Old English Metre ', *Early English and Norse Studies Presented to Hugh Smith in Honour of his Sixtieth Birthday*, pp. 150–71, edd. A. Brown and P. Foote (London, 1963).

J. C. Pope, *The Rhythm of Beowulf: An Interpretation of the Normal and Hypermetric Verse Forms in Old English Poetry*, Revised ed. (New Haven and Oxford, 1966).

J. B. Bessinger and P. H. Smith, *A Concordance to Beowulf* (Ithaca, 1969).

7 Archaeology *

S. Pfeilstucker, *Spätantikes and germanisches Kunstgut in der früh-angel-sächsischen Kunst* (Berlin, 1936).

S. Lindqvist, ' Sutton Hoo and Beowulf ', *Antiquity*, XX (1946).

R. L. S. Bruce-Mitford, ' The Sutton Hoo ship-burial. Recent theories and some comments on general interpretation '. *Proceedings of the Suffolk Institute of Archaeology*, XXV, *pp. 1–78 (1949)*.

D. E. Martin Clark, ' Significant objects at Sutton Hoo ', *Early Cultures of North West Europe* (Chadwick Memorial Volume) ed. Cyril Fox and Bruce Dickins, pp. 109–19 (Cambridge, 1950).

R. L. S. Bruce-Mitford, The Snape boat-grave. *Proceedings of the Suffolk Institute of Archaeology*, XXVI (1952).

R. C. Cramp, ' Beowulf and Archaeology ', *Medieval Archaeology*, I, pp. 57–77 (1957).

---

* A definitive account of the Sutton Hoo ship-burial is to be published in four volumes by the British Museum. Vol. I is in the press. The papers on Sutton Hoo subjects by R. L. S. Bruce-Mitford cited above, including others referred to in the footnotes in Chapter IV, are to be reprinted in book form (*Sutton Hoo Studies*).

H. R. Ellis Davidson, *The Sword in Anglo-Saxon England* (Oxford, 1962).

Map of Britain in the Dark Ages, 2nd edition, H.M. Ordnance Survey (Chessington, 1966).

C. L. Wrenn, ' Sutton Hoo and Beowulf ', Supplement to *Beowulf* by R. W. Chambers, pp. 508–23 (1967). (See Bibliography, Section 5, Interpretation and Criticism, under R. W. Chambers.)

H. R. Ellis Davidson, ' Archaeology and Beowulf ' in Garmonsway and Simpson (see Bibliography, Section 4, Translations, G. K. Garmonsway and J. Simpson) (1968).

C. Green, *Sutton Hoo, The Excavation of a royal ship-burial* (London, 2nd edition, 1968).

R. L. S. Bruce-Mitford, *The Sutton Hoo Ship-burial : A Handbook* (British Museum, the latest edition). (First edition, 1968.)

Rupert and Myrtle Bruce-Mitford, ' The Sutton Hoo lyre, Beowulf and the origins of the frame-harp ', *Antiquity*, XLIV, pp. 7–13 (1970).

B. Hope-Taylor, *Yeavering* (H.M. Stationery Office, London, forthcoming).

INDEX

Apocope, 15 f., 18 ff., 23 f.
Archaisms, 3, 5, 14
Armour, 38 ff., 88 ff.
Attila, Burial of, 36

Back-mutation, 11
Bahuvrīhi compounds, 6 f.
Beow and Grendel, 77 f.
Beowulf, Age of, 64, 72 f.
— Historical existence of, 58, 73 ff.
— Superhuman feats of, 59, 62, 74 ff., 82 f.
Beowulf, Composita in, 4 ff.
— Date of, 10, 18 f., 23 ff., 86–9, 96 ff.
Bernicia, Origin of, 52 ff.
Britons and English, 54 f.

Cædmon, *Beowulf* and, 13, 25
Celtic element in Northumbria, 54 f.
Christianity, 24 f., 32, 49 f.
Christian poetry, Origin of, 13 f.
Compounds in poetry, 4 ff.
Conventional phraseology, 9, 17 f.
Corselets, 40, 88 ff.
Cremation, 32 f., 35 ff.
Cuchulain, 29, 59 f.
Cultural conditions, 27, 40 ff.

Danish history, 64 ff.
Demonstrative, Function of the, 23

Dialecticism in poetry, 5, 8 f., 11 ff.
Dialects, Anglo-Saxon, 7 f.
Dragon's treasure, The, 32, 37 ff.

Early forms, 14 ff.

Finnsburh, 31, 45, 48
Franks Casket, Carvings on the, 40 ff.
— — Language of the, 20 ff.

Geat history, 69 ff.
Gold, Profusion of, 38, 41
Grave-mounds, Plundering of, 38
Grendel in England, 77 f.
Grettissaga, 57 ff.

h, Loss of, 16 f., 19 f.
Helmets, 38 ff., 94
Heroic poetry, Character of, 8, 30 ff.
hild(e)- in composition, 19
Historical parallels, 44, 48 f., 68, 74, 80 ff. *See also* Attila and Russ chieftain
Homer, 29 ff., 36 f.

Inorganic vowels, 15, 18, 20

Kingship, 40, 42, 46 ff., 81 f.

Late forms, 9 f.
Lays, Germanic and Anglo-Saxon, 30 f.